AF574734

Unlawful Assembly

LUCY MCKENZIE & ALAN MICHAEL

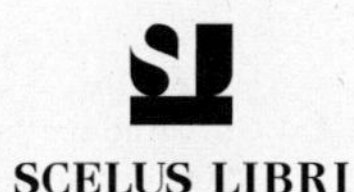

Shooting Diary by Lucy McKenzie
The Nagging Flower, Magic Realism and Not Going To Lie by Alan Michael
Foreword to the first edition by Martin McGeown and Ed Atkins

Cover image by Josephine Pryde
Cover model: Marta Fontolan
Graphic design by HIT
Shooting Diary edited by Ray McKenzie
Scelus Libri logo by Christian Flamm
Printed by DZA Druckerei zu Altenburg GmbH in an edition of 800

First published in an edition of 150 for Volcano Extravaganza: Evil Under The Sun, Stromboli, 2013 with the support of the Fiorucci Art Trust

Second edition published by Koenig Books, London

Koenig Books Ltd
At the Serpentine Gallery
Kensington Gardens
London W2 3XA
www.koenigbooks.co.uk

ISBN 978-3-86335-490-9

Printed in Germany

Distribution:

Buchhandlung Walther König, Köln
Ehrenstr. 4, 50672 Köln
Tel. +49 (0) 221 / 20 59 6 53
Fax +49 (0) 221 / 20 59 6 60
verlag@buchhandlung-walther-koenig.de

Switzerland
AVA Verlagsauslieferungen AG
Centralweg 16
CH-8910 Affoltern a.A.
Tel. +41 (44) 762 42 60
Fax +41 (44) 762 42 10
verlagsservice@ava.ch

Outside Europe
D.A.P. / Distributed Art Publishers, Inc.
155 6th Avenue, 2nd Floor
USA-New York, NY 10013
Fon +1 (0) 212 627 1999
Fax +1 (0) 212 627 9484
eleshowitz@dapinc.com

UK & Eire
Cornerhouse Publications
70 Oxford Street
GB-Manchester M1 5NH
Fon +44 (0) 161 200 15 03
Fax +44 (0) 161 200 15 04
publications@cornerhouse.org

Contents

Foreword
Note To Self

Text and image; image and text. Paintings that use commercial techniques to trick and seduce; stories that captivate by their formulaic construction. The connection between systematic painting and genre fiction is in the use of crafted effect—whether for dramatic tension or illusory depth—in a way that is, at the very least, plausible. This connection isn't a metaphor, merely a parallel. Lucy McKenzie and Alan Michael have familiarised themselves with the methodologies of illusionistic painting, *trompe l'oeil* and photorealism respectively. They step in and out of these processes, repeatedly returning to gaze at the surfaces they have invoked, sometimes presented in direct contrast.[1] Their paintings are conventional, formal and time-consuming; qualities used to reinforce their intentions in a way that could not be achieved by simply presenting an object or photograph rather than its hand-painted stand-in.

1 McKenzie and Michael have shown together on several occasions since their meeting in 1995 at Duncan of Jordanstone College of Art and Design in Dundee. In 2009, for the exhibition *The Associates* in Dundee, Michael's photorealist paintings were hung inside a *trompe l'oeil* room décor by McKenzie, their different manipulation of illusionistic surface shown one inside the other.

Crime fiction has a prescribed structure: the consumer of crime paperbacks demands both novelty and the reassurance of being in familiar territory. But its typology is versatile and open to mutation, so that new crime fiction categories are created when its parameters are transgressed. Its rules can be studied, learned and then inhabited without disturbing its populist surface. Detective fiction can therefore be instrumentalised as a paradigm of procedure. This procedure is often constructed so well as to make it dissolve in the pleasure of experience, and, like many orthodoxies, it is routinely taken for granted. Why is poison always considered a 'woman's weapon'? Why does the market demand that the people on the covers of books should have so little in common with the characters they are meant to embody?

But what about a crime paperback as a piece of site-specific work, where the location of the action and the place in which it is read are one and the same? *Unlawful Assembly* is a collection of interrelated short stories that was intended as a cheap holiday read to titillate and entertain visitors to the Mediterranean island of Stromboli. The target readership were the participants in and visitors to an event entitled *Evil Under the Sun*, which took place there in the summer of 2013.[2] McKenzie and Michael's intention for the event was to produce an *adequate object*—a book of neat, functioning narratives that could seamlessly integrate into the scenery and

2 *Volcano Extravaganza* is an annual informal residency and festival on the island of Stromboli hosted by The Fiorucci Art Trust since 2010. Its 2013 programme, *Evil Under the Sun*, was curated by Lucy McKenzie and the Trust's director Milovan Farronato. *Unlawful Assembly* was published by the Trust in collaboration with the artist's imprint Scelus Libri.

props of a civilised society at leisure. The extended tale by McKenzie, 'Shooting Diary', is a self-contained account of a murder on the volcano. The trio of short stories by Alan Michael—'The Nagging Flower', 'Magic Realism' and 'Not Going to Lie'—are interwoven by a repetition of themes, phrases and characters; Stromboli itself appears alternately in distant reports or as the setting for events. The four stories are united not only by the book's sequential order, but by their shared themes of narcissism, ineffectuality and paranoia. Stromboli's identity is irrevocably bound to the film of the same name made by Roberto Rossellini in 1950. *Unlawful Assembly* uses the island as the backdrop for its own cinematic viewpoint: the watching and making of films is acted out by their protagonists from a variety of obscure angles. The explicit link between film, literature and crime was identified by Alain Robbe-Grillet and the *nouveau roman* writers and their appropriation of detective fiction subverted the genre's original function, bringing it into the lexicon of the literary avant-garde.

As with the *nouveau roman*, McKenzie and Michael's handling of the detective form is deliberately superficial. By styling their atmospheres to those evoked by crime fiction, they turn *Unlawful Assembly* into an intermediary between fiction and art. As a collaboration between two painters, the project was explicitly approached as a means of generating a more complex form of visual content than could be achieved merely by illustrating their texts: collaboration itself was the goal, with a format chosen to follow suit. Both artists use appropriation, at times treating their source material with the same casualness as crime fiction's dealings with death, where it is trivialized it into a clue-generated narrative device.

Both painters also have an often ambiguous relationship with their chosen subjects, acknowledging that appropriation can be a form of colonisation. In their hands it is a perverse ally.

Following on from the publication of *Unlawful Assembly*, and reducing their collaborative experience to a form of 'found material', the artists went on to create a series of paintings and photographs for the exhibition *Note To Self* at The Artist's Institute in New York.[3] Alan Michael's painting *Gases Rising* is based on photography of generic vinyl exhibition signage, here representing a bespoke sign re-using typography designed by HIT, Berlin, for the original cover design of *Unlawful Assembly*. The style of the painting alludes to the focal-depth and reflection fetishes of classical photorealist painters —a mindless value system according to the visual representation of labour, and a potentially endless and shallow surface fabric that provides a space-filling analogue to the extremely conservative procedural formalism of crime fiction. Lucy McKenzie's *Quodlibet XXVII (Unlawful Assembly I)* is a traditional *trompe l'oeil* pin-board arrangement. Historically, these paintings were used for the discreet expression of political or religious dissent. McKenzie's, however, are more like the ubiquitous research mind-maps of DVD boxset *policier* dramas, indispensable to both detective and sociopath alike. It shows ephemera relating to the writing of *Shooting Diary* such as an email from one of her fictional protagonists to Alan Michael, and the on-line payment form for a private Crime Fiction Academy in New York. One of the

3 *Note To Self,* The Artist's Institute, New York, September 20th–October 20th 2013.

objects it contains is the 1975 Penguin edition of *The Mandelbaum Gate* by the Scottish author Muriel Spark.

Muriel Spark wrote about surveillance, blackmail and betrayal within isolated groups such as nuns and expatriates. Her 1970 novel *The Driver's Seat* is celebrated as a 'reverse detective novel'.[4] In it the central character Lise is simultaneously detective, murderer and victim. In the 1970s, Penguin republished Muriel Spark's back catalogue with a set of contemporary covers featuring specially commissioned photographs by 'Van Pariser'. They are in the then-fashionable style of David Hamilton, but as if his girl-children had grown up into vacant adult women. The soft-focus effect implies romance first and foremost, but also a kind of absentmindedness; the opposite of the head-screwed-on self-sufficiency and dispassionate sexuality that normally typify Spark's protagonists and heroines. What is she dreaming about? As with a great many mass-market book jackets, this series gives the impression of being done on a low-budget, deadline-led production line, with only a cursory knowledge of the novel's setting and plot being deemed necessary to inform the commercial artist's work. McKenzie and Michael collaborated with the conceptual artist Josephine Pryde to produce a special portrait to accompany the reproduction of their stories in this volume. This cover image explicitly embodies the disconnection between the book's characters and their visual representation. By this means they insert their book into that series of Spark reprints, and the world of the genderised paperback populated by vague, Vaseline-lens maidens.

4 Maria Vara, 'The Victim and Her Plots: the function of the overpowering victim in Muriel Spark's *The Driver's Seat*', in David Herman (ed.), *Muriel Spark: twenty-first-century perspectives* (Baltimore, Md.: Johns Hopkins University Press, 2010).

It was in Italy where Patricia Highsmith's anti-hero Tom Ripley learned the rudiments of impersonation and killing, and it is a photograph, both enigmatic and prosaic, taken by Spark in Florence in 1988, that serves as the blueprint for McKenzie's photographic series *Stromboli*. The series is a contemporary update of Spark's middle-class literary milieu, but the scene is the same; the anonymous figures are the readership of *Unlawful Assembly*. Spark and Highsmith shared a cat, Spider, and were among several writers the artists discussed while holidaying on Stromboli in 2012. McKenzie explains:

Alan and I have similar tastes when it comes to literature; we like precision, dreamy hysteria and exploitation. Over time the recommendation and discussion of books created a sublimated intimacy between us. On Stromboli with a group of friends last summer I got to sketch his portrait, another form of redirected affection. On the sunny terrace he was reading accounts of secret Zionist cells in Palestine; I read about Stephen Ward's part in the Profumo Affair of 1963. Ward used drawing to weasel his way into the lives of useful people, which made me reflect on my own motivations for drawing from life. It seemed like a good fiction. In 'Shooting Diary' the gang are attempting to make an 'artsploitation' film, while one of their group, a Ripleyesque sociopath, uses flattering portraiture as a tool for social climbing. My drawings of Alan were the precursors to his.

Like the ratio in fast food of fat, salt and sugar to protein, their stories confront pathology in a consumable (and cynical) package of calibrated sex, violence and humour. Alan Michael's stories are embedded within one another with dreamy circularity. They play with concealment and observation, and the mind-set of a cursory, received knowledge of crime fiction, as picked up from TV films and themed fashion spreads. In 'The Nagging Flower' we descend into a description of a graphic novel while still within a film showcasing a loosely-styled incarnation of a famous literary detective (as well as several different films in which the character has starred before, styled just as badly). It's been said that the structure of a police investigation replicates the technique of the modern novel: 'there are clues to an event, say a murder, and someone comes along and puts the pieces together in order that truth may be revealed'.[5] Michael makes his own use of this; the unstable, barely rendered characters in his three stories exist in an atmosphere of conspiracy and reference to real events and actual crimes, but here investigation remains unfulfilled, 'non-resolved'. The process being described is the activity of the appearance itself, the image of *Crime Fiction*. Codes are inoperable labels.

McKenzie's rigorously plotted and structured longer story, processes her themes through an absorption and deployment of these codes situated at the boundary between simulation and the self-consciously skilled industry of genre writers. The structure becomes invisible as the story moves ahead and the fates of her characters loom larger than the knowledge that this is a component of a visual art practice. Her protagonists express the same casually misogynistic opinions as those found in the novels of Agatha Christie and PD James. Using dialogue gleaned from websites such as *overheardinnewyork*, their exchanges are disconcertingly conventional, as if the artist is trying to inhabit attitudes as far away from her own as

5 Alain Robbe-Grillet Interview, *The Art of Fiction*, Paris Review, No. 99, Spring 1986.

possible. She challenges the reader to separate what she says from what she thinks.

In the scene she sets, her characters experience art as a lifestyle choice in which sexuality is a simplified, mundane decor. Fundamentally, 'Shooting Diary' attempts to explore the failure and disjunction that occurs when sexuality, skilfully evoked through prose, is translated to a concrete visual form like cinema. Those who deal in the erotic succeed only in this when the rules of pornography (rules just like crime fiction's, both rigid and permeable) are recognized. The experiments of the *nouveau roman* writers are a case in point.

Agatha Christie's *The Mousetrap* is the longest running play of all time. People who don't visit the theatre very often might find its on-stage illusion of snowstorms raging beyond country house windows more convincing than its dialogue, acting and plot. The overheating in the theatre may even send them to sleep. Stromboli is such a stage. It is an island where the police work out, wear tight shirts and drive around in golf-carts. People there observe a code of dressed-down, off-duty money with a supporting crew of seasonal service workers. The total elimination of the chaos back on the mainland provides the essential conditions for the colonisations of genre and format in the following texts.

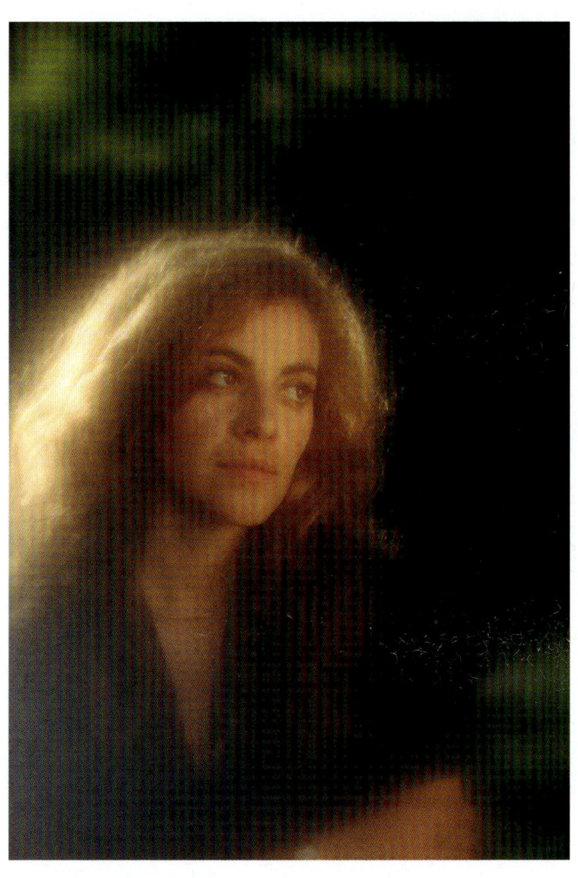

Josephine Pryde
Unlawful Assembly (Cover Art Print), 2013,
pigmented inkjet print, Courtesy RSFA

Shooting Diary
Chapter 1

First let's look at Mercedes' eyes. She is gazing up intently so we have a clear view of them, and for once she is not wearing her sunglasses. They are the most remarkable thing about her face; not because of their shape, size or distance from each other, which are all standard issue, but because they are a deep cornflower blue flecked with violet. A photograph of her with red eye from the flash is something to behold. At this moment her eyes are crossed comically because she is examining the tips of her hair, held up to the light and in contrast to the sky. This bad habit, in which she can be absorbed for hours, is to check for split ends, a plight she suffers from terribly, especially here with the relentless sunshine and sea salt. She surveys the handful, picks out some culprits and snaps off the ends. Then she scoops another fistful of the Earl Grey-coloured stuff and begins again.

Teta emerges from the beach-house, plops down on the sun lounger beside her and without missing a beat whacks Mercedes' hand so the hair falls.

"You told me to do that if you started that stupid habit again. It's infectious; I will also do it now even though my hair was cut last week by the best hairdresser on Wilshire."

"Too kind," Mercedes replies, crossing her arms over her broad chest. "What's going on in there?"

"Still dusting."

Through the doorway of the beach-house behind them the interior is shrouded in gloom but it is clear from the sound of low voices and other intermittent noises that there are people moving purposefully inside.

Squinting over lowered sunglasses, Teta starts to handle the tips of her hair in exactly the same way. Her eyes are pale and greenish and her hair is the colour of custard. Two figures lounging on a beautifully informal terrace, strewn with magazines, bottles of mineral water and swimming paraphernalia. Here they are, soaking up the late afternoon sun and humming to their ipods as the sea laps only a few meters away.

Normally, they would only be seen wearing expertly applied make-up and with immaculate hair, but now they have the bleak and unkempt look of most women in their natural state. They sometimes twist on their loungers to watch what is happening inside. Baking in the heat, they occasionally pass comment. Through the genteel chit-chat a subject develops, gradually becoming more focused until they are pulling out their headphones and sitting up, looking around the terrace in a determined manner. The taller one, Mercedes, enters the house and a few minutes later returns with a spiral bound pad of blank paper and a pencil case. They move to a nearby dining table and organize it into a work desk.

Both are now drawing, silently and with great concentration. After ten minutes they examine each other's results and Teta says:

"Is that how you draw?"

"What do you mean?"

"Are you drawing in a certain style or is that how you draw?"

"I don't know what you mean… this is how I draw. It's not good or what?"

"No, it's not that. Is that how you mean to do it or is that just how it comes out?"

"I'm not sure…"

They are both sketching the same thing. Though their styles are noticeably different it is clear that what they are conjuring on the sheets is the same subject. We can see that Teta has had no formal training—actually has no idea at all how to draw. She has started and stopped, sipped water, taken new sheets of paper. She has changed the size of the face several times, finally settling on something small that hovers in the middle of the paper. Mercedes, on the other hand, has worked slowly on the same sheet, methodically marking out the symmetry line down the middle of the face, placing the levels for the eyes, the bottom of the nose and the centre of the lips. She has an eraser in one hand and constantly modifies the faint lines as she makes them. What emerges as her marks get darker and more precise is a long angular face with a glaring expression and a brush of dark spikey hair. It is a very masculine face, cruel, with a strong jaw and cheekbones, but it rests on an overly thin neck.

"I think his eyes are closer together, see, the way I have drawn him," says Teta.

"Mmm. What's hard to show is the colour of his skin. That's what makes his eyes glitter and his teeth shine out so much. They are very white aren't they? He hardly ever smiles."

Teta makes no response to this. She has stopped

drawing, and is now sitting on her hands in a posture of defeat. Instead she makes quiet suggestions for improvements. Under her direction the taller woman corrects the eyes, adds eyelashes and shapely eyebrows, a cleft in the chin and a five o'clock shadow.

"You could make a skin tone by rubbing it with your finger."

"No, that's not allowed. They know he's an Arab anyway."

Mercedes puts down her pencil and turns to face Teta, confident from the success of her drawing. "You know I don't think I ever saw you talk or even look at him until the other evening. I'm surprised you know so much about his appearance."

Teta avoids the accusation by scrutinising the drawing as if it is a fascinating first edition lithograph. "What did Orran do for the skin then?"

"Orran never drew him."

"What? I don't believe it. I thought that he drew everyone."

"Not at all. It looks like that but he doesn't."

Teta thinks. "His drawing of me made me like him more. It made me feel special, as if he was the only one of you who cared about who I really am. You all just see the superstar. I could tell him things from the past I usually never speak about. Is that bad?"

"No. It's just drawing. He's not killing anyone. He always tries his best and that's what's important."

* * *

Teta was not the only person who had enjoyed the attention and portraiture of Orran Kirby in that fateful week. He had been sketching Gustav Klem on the night Hannah's fate was sealed. That June night had had the last breezes before the airlessness of high summer had hit in earnest. We see Hannah turn off the busy main square and into the steep narrow path that is the start of the route up the volcano. She is in the same white tennis dress she had worn that afternoon for the knock-about in the grounds of the rehabilitation clinic with doctors Davda and Anselmo. Thinking of those quaint ladies she turns and surveys the bay below her: there was the beach-side clinic, with all the patients safely tucked up in bed already no doubt. *Those sagacious psychiatrists would not approve of where she was going now, that's for sure!* She turns off this path onto a smaller more secluded track, and as she approaches a modern gate she becomes cautious. She looks up the driveway lined with herbaceous borders at the anonymous villa, piecing together a map in her mind from the anecdotal information Mimmo has given her. Before we know it, she has silently scaled the gate, vaulted over and is walking up the path, keeping to its shadier corners. Her hem brushes against gelsomino and bougainvillea, and a courteous tabby cat lets her pass undisturbed.

The façade of the house is blank; the entrance is on another side. There are only a few small windows, but on top there is a roof terrace, with vines and creepers trailing over the parapet. As she approaches the building the faint sound of music can be made out, so the image has now acquired a soundtrack. Not that she realises it is music at first—it sounds more like a slowed-down fire alarm in the distance—but by the time she is close enough to touch the façade of the villa with her fingertips a melody has emerged. It is what can best be described as

'Haunted House'—the meandering, unfocused, echoey organ music assigned to anything spooky. She loves this sound, in combination with the breeze and the warm shadows cast by the artificially lit maritime pines. *No wonder Orran and Morgane would rather hang out up here than with us down there.* The low voices and clinking glasses that can be made out over the music suggest there is a small private party going on, not only on the terrace above, but in the courtyard that Mimmo had described to her. She presses her back and palms to the concrete surface of the building and edges towards the laughter and organ music. As she approaches a corner she can tell that people are very close, but hidden on the other side.

She is reminded of a family trip to Oslo, and the low-relief sculpture she saw on the façade of the town hall. There were three figures: on the side facing the bay were a man and woman holding hands, but the woman was reaching round the corner to stroke the hand of another man hidden from view. She always considered this a confusingly racy motif for a civic building. But why did she feel so inclined to reminisce these last days? Perhaps it was because, a month shy of her seventeenth birthday, she was about to grow up, and childhood experiences were starting to take on greater meaning as thoughts and feelings started to loop round into new ones.

Pressed against the corner, Hannah can hear the conversation clearly enough now to know the speakers are talking fluent Mandarin. There is an outdoor shower beside her, and the tinted glass that encloses it reflects what is around the corner. Two European men stand in shorts and polo shirts. They are talking in this language to mask their discussion from the other house guests, who are dotted around a tidy courtyard edged with backlit foliage of aloe vera and agave. Some of the guests are watching a large video projection that she now realises is the source of the music. But these two men are talking business.

The glass surface of the shower cabin is perfect, so she has a mirror in which to examine the terrace. The people are middle-aged and dressed very simply, mostly seen in silhouette against the video projection, which looks like a computer game but is actually a CGI journey through a reconstruction of Pompeii. A cluster of people are approached by a stocky Middle Eastern man who serves drinks. *Could he be a friend of Shirhan?* A non-descript head near her nods vigorously, and she recognises this as one of the stock gestures of Orran. He is sitting close by with the Swiss banker Gustav Klem, the owner of the villa. Glasses of Aperol Spritz sit on the low table in front of them, next to some of Orran's conventional nude studies of Klem. Unlike the men with the impressive Mandarin, they are having a conversation she can understand.

"Holidays are a sore point," Orran sniffs.

"Oh?"

"I can never get away from the gallery."

"Hmm?"

"It's always so hectic."

"Uhuh."

"The new project, it's taking time to set up and all my cash is tied up in it. I'm expecting a lump sum pretty soon, but until then I'm at the grindstone. It's a strange way of conducting one's life isn't it, lurching from one situation to the next?" Orran laughs, trying to appear casual.

Orran, the charming all-American autocrat thinks Hannah. She knows where he expects that money from; the suspicions recently formed in her connective brain are confirmed.

"Believe it or not, but this is not what I would call a scintillating evening," Gustav eyes Orran intently. "Fancy a dip?"

"Mmm. Maybe." Orran fishes in his pocket for his iphone. After several Aperols he has dropped his guard, and has started to talk about his financial situation. But he has felt the pull of Hannah's mind, the sudden awareness of a probing consciousness lurking nearby. Using the phone's polished surface he sees her small white face reflected in the shower unit behind him. The expression in her eyes shocks him. It was, he remembered later, as if she was playing some dangerous game. If there was anyone on this island more devious than him it was her; he has a presentiment of trouble.

His blank expression meets hers, but suddenly the white face disappears. A hairy hand has grabbed her bum and a leather-clad arm has hooked round her waist pulling her backwards. She giggles to disguise the tremor of fear running through her, hoping Mimmo won't expose her to Orran and the partygoers on the patio. But he won't, their affair is a secret. "Where have you been hiding?" She wriggles round. "I've been hiding," she whispers, and leads him away from the house down into the bushes.

* * *

There. What do you think?" says Mercedes. Her drawing is complete.

"It's him. But the neck is too thin," Teta replies. Mercedes turns and waves to the man who has put his head out of the beach-house's doorway. He ducks under the police tape and approaches. He is of average height, very deeply tanned and wears a short-sleeved blue shirt and black trousers with a red stripe down the sides.

Mercedes proffers the sketchpad and speaks in an Italian that has the same boarding-school proficiency as her portraiture. "Here is a drawing, officer. We have no photographs of Sirhan, only this."

"*Grazi signorina*. We will circulate it immediately."

Shooting Diary
Chapter 2

He looks nothing like the sinister caricature; the pathological killer with a rich glint of lunacy flashing in his eyes. No. His face may be angular but it is undersized, and his expression is not at all malicious. He gives off the impression of being a young man who moves forward through life one day at a time, without thinking very much about things; a bit like most people. He is small and delicate, not much more than a boy, perhaps aged between twenty and twenty-four. His skin is dark and luminous, burnished by centuries of prenatal sun. He is sweating profusely.

The Lipari police caught him trying to sneak onto a SNAV to Naples, not because of the drawing but because he was behaving suspiciously. Posters of a murderer had been pasted around the island with *Sirhan Nafisi: ricercato per omicidio* written underneath Mercedes' drawing. His stealthy creep had been in such contrast to the easy-going manner of the people around him on the pier as they lounged around waggling coloured plastic buckets and ice-creams that he had been easy to spot. Now, handcuffed to a wrought-iron garden chair, it looks like his prosaic forward progress has come to an ineluctable standstill.

"How come you're dressed like that?" Sophie asks him. He does not respond. He is being held at Gustav Klem's villa. The local police had phoned their contact Mimmo to ask if the investigations could be based there while the beach-house was checked for forensic evidence; the local police station was inadequate for so much activity. This evidence was being sporadically sent to the path lab in Messina. There are investigating officers from the local police, from Lipari and from the Messina police representing the district of Sicily.

There are more police swarming over the island now than there has ever been in its entire history. More were summoned because by coincidence there has been a break-in at Mimmo's sister Chiara's animal shelter. The Russian diplomat who has been a guest at the villa has vanished too, leaving behind a sick bulldog. No-one is suggesting that evil now suddenly prowls in every shadow on the island; it is more likely that a disjointed chain of misunderstandings has begun to unfold, each unfortunate incident occurring independently of the others. Even Hannah's death was surely nothing more than a stupid accident. The tourists are starting to make other plans, setting off for Panarea, Vulcano and Alicudi.

"Why is he dressed like that?" Sophie asks Chiara. Sophie has a vein pulsing in her forehead and she picks at a scab on her lip.

"*Quali sono questi vestiti?*" Chiara asks Sirhan.

"*La polizia mi ha dato questi vestiti di merda da indossare mentre si controllano miniera*" he replies in a flat tone.

"He says the police gave him these shit clothes while they examine his. They need to test them for evidence, and check his story..."

"What is his story?"

"He says actually nothing; just that he didn't do nothing."

Sirhan looks outlandish in the shiny day-glow tracksuit that has replaced the linen djellaba he usually wears. The male and female cops are milling around; so are occasional bath-robed house guests, none of whom seem to mind this interruption to their routine. The different social groups cross each other in front of Sirhan oblivious to each other, like sharks in a tank. A crate containing a sculpture, also day-glow coloured, is being unpacked in the middle of the courtyard and the Pompeii video is switched off. Gustav and his business partners lunch on the balcony above and survey the scene.

"Tell them to mind the sculpture!" somebody shouts down.

The sun is melting Sirhan's cranium. A few feet from him a woman has slipped off her robe and is using the recently installed smoked glass outdoor shower. Through its brown transparency you can see she is smirking. Chiara leads Sophie to a corner of the terrace.

"If she was killed on Friday, like they think, he could have done it. His friend Massoud is the housekeeper here. Massoud says he turned up early on Saturday morning, very upset about something… and the path outside is the one leading to the volcano, where she was found."

Several Lipari police arrive and approach the local officers standing by Sirhan. Sophie shifts uncomfortably, trying not very effectively to conceal a great deal of distress. Chiara cocks her head, listening. "I think they say that they found traces of Hannah's DNA on his clothes, and that the bruises on her throat match his hands. They even know that she was strangled by a left-handed person. *Allora*, it was him. *Incredibile!"*

"Did he tell Massoud anything?" Sophie looks even more distressed, as if she is camouflaging something that cannot be kept so for much longer. She fiddles compulsively with the strap of the video camera over her shoulder.

"He was crying, but wouldn't talk. He's been in Massoud's room watching television till Massoud told him there were wanted posters with his name under a drawing of Colonel Gaddafi all around the island."

Sophie stares at Chiara then at the cluster of officers gathered in the shade and then back at Chiara. She walks towards them, across the sun-soaked courtyard. She stops halfway, lingers by Sirhan, who looks at her with the same abject misery she saw on Friday evening. This time it is directly in her eyes and not mediated by the camera's lens. She turns back to Chiara. "Chiara! Will you translate for me?"

The two women approach the police. Sophie says she has something to show them and holds out her video camera. They cluster around the little fold-out monitor and she winds till she locates the spot she is looking for. The police go silent. Several turn around and look at Sirhan. Sirhan looks up at the minty sky, then at the paving stones; a drop of sweat lands on them. The police take the camera from Sophie's hands, talking volubly among themselves, starting to dial their mobile phones, waving them in the air for reception. Sophie reaches for her camera as it disappears from view.

"Tell them I need the camera! For filming..." Chiara shakes her head. The police fire a barrage of questions at Sophie in incomprehensible Italian. Chiara says "Now it's evidence they say. And what will you film? They are taking it directly to the police station to show the detective interviewing Wim."

After some debate between Chiara and the police, Sirhan's handcuffs are removed and he calls for Massoud. Massoud comes over from the gate at the entrance to the property where he has been waiting to be beckoned; their packed bags are at his feet. Now Sirhan is a swishing blur of bright yellow. As he leaves the courtyard he turns to look angrily at Sophie, who sees him framed by the tall straight maritime pine trees. Then he is gone.

The Nagging Flower

The big red quad poster of William Wyler's 'Les Grandes Espaces' is outside the lobby. First thing tomorrow morning they'll change that to 'La Prisonnière'. Large disembodied lips floating beneath chains. We pay for our tickets and climb the stairs in silence, passing along the cool corridors of the old theatre. Through the scuffed swing-doors with circular windows and into the huge auditorium, dark brown with worn velvet seats. The little faint spotlights on the ceiling are supposed to look like stars. Nobody's near us in the rows surrounding so we could talk if we wanted to, all sound just dies in here. It's so empty in this cinema, always just a few students. The perfect place for us to sleep, in a big dark space, hopefully all night. Be on your guard and keep a low profile, Baptiste says, they are noting what we do, spying, observing us all the time. She says they want to eat us with their eyes! In the seat beside me, Baptiste is still holding on tight to my boyfriend's briefcase, full of its dynamite, his files on politicians and the special map of the city, the dice.

But following the production company's logo —misty clouds parting, initials gliding together across a starry sky, a winged goddess presenting a wreath, and then the whole thing transformed into a schematic monochrome version of the final configuration—there's a slow zoom, like in older Italian movies, then a succession of zooms. It's a sequence showing the summit of a steep mountain, covered in debris, rocks and ash. Its filmed more in the style of an old horror film, where the zoom might typically come with a sudden blast of orchestral music just in case you missed the yawning skull exposed in the newly turned soil of the graveyard. This graveyard would look as if it had been created in the studios of the company specialising in these trashy English films, by technicians familiar with those requirements. My father would complain that the blood is far too red.

The camera is panning left-right, right-left, up-down, down-up, capturing explosions of rocks and sparks, followed by a small mushroom cloud of ash. The zoom now begins and combines with a gentle pan to the left, slowly building, before ending its trajectory. There's a booming noise, a far-off explosion, this time only on the soundtrack. And the zoom speeds up, increasing until the subject is in extreme close up, a man's face, raising his head into the frame, looking up intensely, squinting at the sun, at something off camera. He's southern and dark with a grimy heavily lined face, a worker, maybe a mechanic. It's obvious the man isn't an important character, his role must be just to embody something. He returns to tinkering with a moped's engine.

The camera zooms and pans, initially from a distance beyond a village by the sea, probably set up on a surrounding hillside. It's establishing a character's entrance to the movie. Now the shot slowly zooms and pans from a position inside the town, perhaps from the window of an upper story apartment. Then—must be from a rooftop—showing again the smoking slopes of the famous volcano above the town in the distance. A dynamic framing of the ash slopes' diagonals dissecting the screen and the camera zooms to the small streets far below. Grainy little people are slowly making their way past souvenir shops and ice cream vendors in the bright sunshine.

Now, at street level, some children in colourful t-shirts are playing football while groups of teenagers sit on the steps of a crumbling stucco baroque church in a small piazza. One of the children kicks the ball out of control and it bounces just in front of a teenager who catches it skilfully in one hand and playfully pretends he might steal it. The little gang of children run up to the teenagers noisily protesting in the film's foreign language. As they reach the older kids a loud rumble is heard and a series of close-ups show heads of various children looking up. A medium distance shot of the volcano's summit shows a grey puff of smoke rising slowly in the pale blue sky.

Motorcycles buzz around. An angled shot from a higher building gives an abstract view of the little square with hikers holding walking sticks crossing the street in all directions followed by the golf buggies that act as taxis on this island. A tour guide assembles the hikers together and leads them off in formation towards the slopes of the volcano. A close-up of the curved interlocking tiles that form the surface of the piazza is used for a backdrop for the titles of the movie, a sequence that takes a few minutes, accompanied by quick tempo piano music, a bit distorted like its been recorded badly. The movie is called 'The Nagging Flower'.

After the director's credit, it cuts to a montage which lets us know there are occasional signs that this town has been the focus of heavily armed warfare some years ago, perhaps more recently, some buildings still have blue polythene and tarpaulin covering gaping holes made by shelling, with mangled metal reinforcement rods poking out from shattered concrete. On the beach, children play in the burned out wreck of a tank, firmly sunk into the black sand, decorated with the peeling stickers of fashion concessions: 'Scelus', 'Pax Gelato', 'Evil Under The Mood' etc. At the outskirts of the town, signs warn of the danger of landmines still hidden across the island. In the harbour, a half submerged rusting ferry, the *Ceca*, rests permanently at a steep angle. Kids jump from the side of the ship into the warm harbour water.

But we don't linger too long on those details and, besides: there's a lot of construction going on. A new hotel is being built on the seafront with foreign development money, the vinyl banners concealing the scaffolding display the insignia of a fictional Chinese property conglomerate. At the harbour, we can see a new passenger terminal building taking shape surrounded by cranes and dusty lorries. As the kids in the water splash around and raucously shout at each other the camera slowly zooms beyond them to reveal a man hanging by the neck from a peeling lifeboat derrick. We don't get to see his face. Padlocked to one of his hands is a holdall dangling and wide open. Whatever might have been in the holdall must have fallen into the sea. A close-up detail of the laminated plastic security pass still attached to his lapel reads "Gareth Williams. MS Intelligence, Geneva—Brand Protection."

* * *

Passengers are disembarking from a hydrofoil at the new jetty. A short, round man emerges from the boat into the sunlight taking care to protect his shoes and directing one of the crew to lift his cases on to the jetty. His costume superficially suggests an old-fashioned look, perhaps the 1950's, or the 1920's, or the 1940's… its unclear which exactly, the wardrobe detailing is a bit cursory. He has a straw hat in the shape of a Homburg but other than the patent shoes and a pocket watch —which he checks with an exaggerated gesture—he is wearing a contemporary pale suit. He smoothes his waxed moustache with gloved fingers. The greying hair is neatly styled but clearly covers his ears. He's got a deep tan and a friendly, expressive face. He might be a comedian, usually seen in broad Italian comedies and farces. Raising a hand to his stomach, he winces and complains to a fellow passenger about something he's eaten during the journey to the island. He dabs his forehead with a handkerchief. His companion, a tall attractive young woman with dark hair and a smart suit, looks at him sympathetically, takes his hand and leads him down the gangway to the pier.

A golf buggy driver is waiting to take them and their luggage to their hotel. He rolls his eyes, grimaces and mutters at the girl-taxi driver with blonde dreadlocks as she cheerfully throws the suitcases into the luggage rack of the buggy. The driver gestures to the man and the woman to take their seats and we see the buggy set off with a sudden jolt causing the man to reach for his hat, exaggerating the movement like a silent movie comedian. As this is happening he is explaining firmly to the woman —despite her pleas—that he is visiting this island strictly in the capacity of a private individual on holiday and has no intention of undertaking any form of detective inquiry. The local Police will be quite capable of dealing with any missing persons cases, he adds, and besides, there need be no reason to think that the woman's friend, Lady Edgware, is responsible for her husband's murder, which, naturally, he was aware of anyway, and had read about in the international papers in Naples and which, of course, may not be a case of murder at all.

The shots dissolve from one to the next, giving a leisurely but progressive feel to the establishment of the setting as the taxi-buggy winds its way through the narrow pathways. But the reckless zooming causes confusion if the viewer isn't familiar with certain types of Italian movies. The title sequence at the beginning made it clear that the money, the crew, the director are Italian. All the sound will be added, the dialogue dubbed later, so everyone can relax just a bit, its a different feel on the set when its a silent take. MOS, it's called.

* * *

The camera zooms around and pans describing and establishing another protagonist's entrance to the movie, introducing him as he rounds a corner. It looks like mid afternoon, very hot. A tired stray dog lying on the pavement looks up as the man, the protagonist, walks across a static shot, from left to right. Maybe it's a comedy? All these zooms—its hard to decide. We see him in close-up, squinting in the direct sunlight. The squint exaggerates a smile of varying degrees that seems to be permanently fixed on his face, despite usually being paired with a severe frown. He looks like someone who pretends to be jolly but who might fly off the handle at the slightest thing. His skin is very pale, he must be about forty, forty-five.

He carries on, turning into a small path between two small office buildings leading to the gate at the back and the glass door of a small apartment block. It's mid afternoon, there's the humming of electric buggies, occasional motorcycles, footsteps, a siren in the distance. Of course, this is all MOS, so these sounds would have been dubbed later. The crew, the money, as mentioned, everything's Italian. Or, certainly, a co-production. He reaches into the pockets of his light blue suit jacket, fishing for some keys. The sun, getting lower, allows the cameras to pick out details in the buildings opposite, shown in short montage studies. We see a small church, badly damaged by the shelling, with plain ground-glass windows, still intact, above a wooden door protected by chained wrought ironwork gates, ornately rendered to resemble ivy branches. The gates form a shallow cage around the door. There's a little sequence focussing on these details before a revealing view of the destroyed interior. Two cats are dozing on a statue of the Virgin lying face down, half buried beneath charred roof beams.

And now he's shown entering the apartment, from inside the room. There's a large window with a door leading to a concrete balcony at one end, at the other a frosted glass partition, the glass frosted in vertical waves, probably dividing the space from the kitchen at the back. In front of the window with the balcony, facing the street, there's a large dark wooden desk covered with glass, a laptop, a printer, drawing materials, papers, scattered on the surface. There's a slow slightly angled tracking shot along the wall of the room to show the pictures on the wall. First, a large photograph of two competing black male sprinters, one in focus, the other blurred, both with their faces hidden in total shadow. Next, a poster of a sweating Christ being secured to his cross just before it is raised to the vertical. This picture looks like a movie still, there's something illegible written at the bottom, probably just the lobby card information. Last, nearest the desk, a framed original artwork by a comic book artist of a colossal ape enveloped in gas, overcome and on the point of collapse. The ape's speech bubble exclaims something in a Cyrillic script.

While we were being shown these details, he's been in the rear of the apartment and comes back without his shirt on, rubbing his neck with a towel, strands of dark hair that were firmly gelled down before now wildly out of place. He's carrying a plate with a sandwich, which he's already eating on the way to his desk. He's got a tattoo on the left side of his chest, a crest with "FK PARTIZAN", in Cyrillic, of course. There's another of the distinctive distant crashing rumbles and he looks up: the volcano is shown puffing its clouds of vapour, framed by the balcony walls. Now, in close up, very large on the screen, we recognise him immediately, nudging each other as if to say "Oh my god, its him!" The actor playing this artist is a notorious former child actor from England who claimed to have been molested on the set of *Bugsy Malone* and has written a book about his experiences, for which he was, naturally, successfully sued. He's changed a lot, physically, of course, even from his later years in adult-roles, having gained weight and lost most of his luxurious dark hair. It's safe to assume he's been cast by the producers because of his messy personal life. His voice will have been dubbed by a foreign actor.

He stretches and sits at his desk. Music fades in on the soundtrack, fast paced electronic music with a melancholic female voice. Now there's a slow tracking shot from the far end of the room, which very gradually closes in on him working briskly and intensely on something. As we get closer, its clear he's working on some drawings. We gather from the style of the drawing that he's probably the artist who produced the artwork of the ape hanging on the wall. Then the shot dissolves into a montage of close ups showing the material he's working on: a comic book story half pencilled, half inked, called 'MILICA!', which, judging by the cover page, is an adult-erotic story of a young woman caught up in a brutal civil war. The artist's name is Bic. We also see scattered pictures of supermodels cut out from magazines, a light box, tracing paper, print-outs of military hardware catalogues and uniforms, print-outs of screencaps from porn movies, and the cd cover of the music which we guess is what's playing on the soundtrack, called 'What Is That In Your Veins?' The camera scans and tracks the frames of the story that Bic's been working on, the arrival of a paramilitary motorized unit at a small town by a river.

The commander is handsome and dark and has a pet albino wolf cub on a chain, alternately straining at its leash and pawing the commander. The men in the unit all have the same black military fatigues and berets with insignia of crowns, triple eagles and wolves surrounded by a rainbow coloured shield shape with the letters 'BPC' at the top. We noticed an actual similar, but slightly different, embroidered badge lying on the artists' desk among the clutter. The unit huddle, salute and quickly disperse to begin destroying the town, firing

RPG rounds into houses and shops, setting fire to small factories. A glossy black armoured bulldozer demolishes a mosque. They round up the men, shooting them or stabbing them to death, their bodies thrown into the rapids of the river below. The camera follows the dramatic lettering of the gunfire 'RATATATATATATAT' snaking across several frames of a page. As this happens, we hear actual sounds of gunfire, echoey and distant. One frame shows, in silhouette with deep red background, a man being raped before he's shot. These scenes are rendered with a lot of what we can see is the artist's signature style of hyper-real 'liquids' and 'smoke'.

The militia have established a base in a local leisure centre. The men have rounded up local women and have brought them to the leisure centre, which has a sign in an eastern language ("Rehabilitacioni centar"). There are heavy tears in the eyes of the women, the cruel pale eyes of the commander gleam as he loosens his belt. Then there's a series of loosely pencilled frames showing violent sex scenes, which are difficult to see because they haven't yet been inked. But we can also see that the artist, Bic, is sentimental and keen to show the tragedy of this terrible civil war. Milica, the beautiful young woman of the title of Bic's story, with her intrepid, wide-set, expressive eyes, thick brows and pouty lips, has been singled out by the commander as being of particular interest. She has become separated from her child and her quest to be reunited will be the motor of the story's plot. The final frame we see her reluctantly remove her headscarf to reveal shining platinum hair.

The volcano rumbles again and Bic stops, looks up to the window.

* * *

Outside the modest seafront hotel the Detective and his companion shield their eyes from the low sun and look up at the volcano's crater. The puff of vapour rises slowly. A porter is taking care of their luggage as the taxi hums into life again and disappears. The camera slowly zooms towards the doors of the hotel from across the street and they both turn to enter the lobby, agreeing to meet in the hotel bar in forty-five minutes. The Detective shakes his head and wags a finger at his shoes, which, despite the short journey to the hotel from the harbour, are covered in fine dust. As the lift doors close to take them from the lobby up to their rooms several Police motorcycles speed past the hotel with their sirens blaring, heading in the direction of the old harbour. We see a low angle shot of the motorcycles turning a corner and passing a vendor selling fresh fish from a portable stall. A customer asks him what this could be about. More forgeries, he says, and resumes his regular cry of "Fres-co!"

Bic's mobile is ringing, the ring tone: gunfire and children screaming. The screen announces an unknown Private Number. Hesitatingly, he answers and has a short conversation only answering no or yes to whatever the distant tinny female voice on the phone is saying. He holds the pose at the end of the conversation for a few seconds, as if frozen, or perhaps just thinking carefully about something. We see a sequence of close-ups, Bic opening a locked drawer under the table, lifting a neat bundle of brand new bank notes. He slips one of the notes out from the bundle and removes a similar, used note from his wallet. From another drawer he lifts out a small black metal box with a slot on one side. We can read the words "SafeScan Portable UV Checker" on the front of the device. He presses a switch and places both notes in turn on the black-light plate of the scanner and, satisfied that both notes show identical green security strips, replaces the notes in the bundle and in his wallet. Gulping the last of his sandwich, he wipes his mouth and then his fingers on his trousers. The bundle is shoved into a plastic bag and he springs out of the chair to put on a shirt and leave.

In the bar of the hotel, the detective and his companion sit at a window overlooking the dusty promenade. A procession of cement mixers and lorries loaded with construction site debris trundle by slowly. The detective rolls his eyes, tuts, sips on a sirop de cassis. He's about to remark about all this upheaval to his companion when we hear the familiar booming sound, and expect to be shown a cutaway of the volcano again but this time it's a shot of debris and rubble from the construction site being dropped down a chute into the back of a lorry. Clouds of dust rise in the evening sun. His companion tilts her glass and rolls the ice and lime around her gin and tonic. She is asking him about a recent case he was involved with. He gently protests but, clearly flattered by this attentive and attractive lady who he really has known only since embarking at Naples, begins to relate the details. She feels her mobile vibrating silently in the pocket of her Capri pants and we see a close up of her furtively glancing at the display, which reads: "1 Message —Bic". With a dazzling smile, she immediately asks him a technical question about the discovery of the victim of this celebrated case, which seems to distract the Detective from making any comment or inquiry about the message on the phone. She reads the message but we don't get to see what it says.

Yes, it was a great strain for me, he says, I prefer to travel just for now, as a private citizen! No more mysteries! There's a montage of scenes showing a compilation of action from a previous movie featuring this character. The grisly discovery of the young cryptologist's body concealed in the holdall; the Metropolitan Police of London baffled at the lack of evidence of intruders; the involvement, at the request of the chief inspector—in blatant defiance of direct orders from the security services—of the great Private Detective, a last throw of the dice.

We see the characters assembled in the private lounge of the luxury hotel as the detective outlines his hypothesis. Again, the Detective is in his superficially old-fashioned costume. The fedora hat—this time dark, hair too long and incorrectly styled for any particular era. Other characters in the drama are not in period costume, and exterior stock establishing shots of the Mayfair street reveal contemporary cars, buildings and advertising.

We can be certain, he says, of this: that for whatever additional reasons—or none, it is not important—Mr. Williams' attitude, demeanour, inquisitive nature, his knowledge, his trusted status at the Ministry were all judged far too much of a risk to someone that his presence could no longer be tolerated. It is obvious to me he wanted to tell someone of what he knew. Alas, his mistake was to forget how ruthless an organization he was working for… A poison—yes! This is what killed him! A poison most likely, of the variety 'amanita phalloides'… if I recall correctly, Professor Hampstead? (Professor Hampstead adjusts his bi-focal spectacles and nods gravely). It was somehow administered on or about the tenth of August, just prior to his final return to Great Britain…

And following a misty dissolve, we see the victim at the American airport, obviously feeling unwell, struggling to sleep during his flight, suffering dizzy spells at the luggage carousel, looking at his tongue in the toilet mirror etc, slumping in the back of the taxi, his face white and sweaty.

The Detective's voiceover continues during this sequence: poor Mr. Williams, he says, realised he had been poisoned a few days later as the effects began to accumulate. He spent some ninety pounds at Harrods —most of it on medication at the pharmacy and not on women's toiletries as leaked to the press by… you, Mr. Wilson! (Mr. Wilson shifts uneasily in his chair and is attempting to maintain an unconcerned expression). I was easily able to trace the source of the information. Mr. Williams pallor clearly captured in the Holland Park filling station video stills from the fifteenth of August are of a man in a very jaundiced and sickly condition… the very typical symptoms of this poison. On the evening of the same day Mr. Williams "colleagues" visited the flat and found Mr. Williams either dead or nearly so. He is defenceless now! They padlocked Mr. Williams into the infamous Northface holdall, and the holdall they placed in the bath, as if the result of a game gone badly wrong. Just the type of predilection Mr. Wilson was so helpfully on hand to suggest to the newspapers (Mr. Wilson smiles and shrugs, resigned). The flat was cleaned, all the medicines removed, not—however—the Harrods receipt, which was somehow missed, a vital clue. Things were arranged just-so for the police to find when asked to check on Mr. Williams. They let themselves out, locking the door after them… Miss Williams, I am convinced your brother was not a transvestite! (Miss Williams dabs her eyes with a handkerchief) And that this is another lurid tale intended to distract us and discredit Mr. Williams, spun by these disgraceful agents of the security services, concocted to veil their wicked actions beneath a cloud of insinuation and smears…

At the word 'cloud' I look up towards the ceiling of the theatre and notice the tiny hazy particles mingling and shining with the moving light beam of the projection. The little stars are twinkling too. I'm reminded of when I was a kid and smoking was permitted at the cinema. Baptiste looks up now too, saying "Marie… I…" and, attempting a weak karate chop movement, slumps beside me. The gas has emerged at precisely the correct moment so that it seems like an effect in keeping with the action of the film, causing confusion rather than alarm. We didn't notice the gas being slowly released into the theatre, through vents in the floor connecting the sex club below, which has been commandeered weeks ago by the secret interior unit of the Security Services, dressed either as sex workers or their bosses. The real sex workers and boss have been cremated, their ashes mixed into the concrete forming the renovations to the Opéra Bastille. The greenish, smoky fumes begin to fill the auditorium overpowering the few people dotted around the room, and have utterly neutralized Baptiste who snores loudly now, I think her tongue is caught in her throat. Her eyes are open.

The Security Service agents, wearing gasmasks and balaclavas, though not obviously armed, take care to walk gently as if concerned not to wake the unconscious audience whose mouths are foaming. Half of them have probably suffocated already. They're shining small silver torches at individuals as they make a sweep, looking for me, Baptiste, Julien's briefcase and the map.

The beam from the projector catches the gases rising slowly through the auditorium. This puts the dot on the 'i', as Baptiste would say. I'm feeling ill and tired and squeeze my eyelids closed for a second, rubbing them, but I can't open them again. An artificial, powerful opium-like substance; a secret chemical agent; a surgical aerosol anaesthetic, an opiate later to be conjectured as weaponized fentanyl. It came either through the fake extra speakers in the walls or it was pumped through the theatre's ventilation system or it simply emerged through pores in the specially fabricated screen of the cinema.

Shooting Diary
Chapter 3

But let's go back a few days to when everyone arrived on Stromboli.

"So the drawings are from photographs?" Mimmo asks, nodding his head admiringly. Wim has removed his work from a leather portfolio and is starting to pin the drawings and watercolours on the walls of the beach-house's large salon, whose French windows lead to the terrace and the Mediterranean beyond. Mimmo met them at the port with a fleet of golf buggy taxis and now everyone is bustling around as they settle in. Sirhan is storing away their suitcases in the cupboard that takes up half of his tiny ground-floor living quarters along with the washing machine and a tall padlocked fridge.

"Yes. The first project was with fashion models. I'd hire them for a week and fly them to Africa for photo sessions. Then I met Mercedes, and through her Hannah, and I started using just them."

"Nice project." Mimmo looks at the drawings. "Where was the shoot for these ones?"

"Congo River."

"The worst part about Africa was that we didn't go out!" says Mercedes at Wim's side, running her hand through his tousled brown hair. "These few were by the beach in Benin," she says pointing with the other hand. "There was literally nothing to buy there. You know the police use bows and arrows in Benin?"

"We did some in Japan too." says Wim.

"I wanted to buy a bonsai tree, but they are so expensive. I don't know about travel. When you think about it, if you've met one person you've basically met everyone," says Mercedes.

"Wim, there's no wifi here." Teta is staring unhappily at her tablet.

"We hope to install it soon; next time you come it will be on," says Mimmo.

"And we shot in Venice, in a graveyard. Venice is a bit like Bruges…" (If Mercedes' brain was a room, one would be forever banging one's shins on the bulky, useless furniture that clutters every corner.)

Teta goes to her room. Morgane joins the group watching Wim hang his pieces of paper haphazardly all over the walls. She says: "The location is very important for his work Mimmo … the explicitly exotic … the adventurism of the nineteenth century. He's like Gauguin … or Rousseau."

"*Si si.* Very nice." Mimmo eyes Hannah standing in the doorway scrutinizing the coastline. With her short hair, she reminds him of a little slave boy.

Orran joins them. He looks fresh and handsome after a shower that has washed away the five-hour ferry ride. He knows everyone except Teta and Sophie, who have both been hired specifically for the filming. The other women had all been at Wim's opening at Xavier Greengrove, the New York Gallery for whom he has been the assistant manager for just under a year (branches also in Shanghai and Berlin; Dubai space opening winter 2013). He had never met Mimmo before, but they had corresponded over the rental agreement and travel arrangements as Greengrove gallery was co-producing the film. Mimmo is the caretaker of several holiday properties on the island, a native recently returned after years living in Columbia.

Sirhan brings them a tray of watermelon juice with crushed ice and mint. Morgane calls the group to gather round and raises her glass to propose a toast. "Ahh, every day is a new and exciting day to make art! It's going to be a beautiful film, Wim. *Bonne chance à tous!*" They all clink glasses.

At this point Orran leaves and heads off to greet those at the villa owned by Gustav Klem and the Swiss consortium who have rented Wim this beach-house. He knows them through the curator Morgane D'angleterre, whose projects they often fund. At the villa he sees Klem and some collectors he knows through Greengrove, couples gay and straight. He gets chatting over a cocktail with a woman who turns out to be a Russian diplomat based in Rome, and invites her to sit for a portrait. He has brought along a sketch pad and pencils just in case an opportunity came up to study someone with a face as interesting as hers. "It's just a hobby, please don't judge me," he assures her bashfully. The likeness he makes of her has a more pronounced jaw line, and he has given a beautiful bounce to her hair. She loves it and he draws another. He also draws her dog, which has had its ear badly scratched by the resident cat Bouffle.

Back down by the beach, Mimmo has stayed for the dinner of fresh salad that Sirhan has prepared, and Sophie has also emerged after her shower and nap. She can be heard laughing heartily on the terrace; she is telephoning her husband and daughter. She has a congenitally loud voice. Chiara had stopped by to welcome them briefly. Mimmo is flirting with the younger women of the group, who he assumes from the drawings will be receptive to his attentions. He leans in and asks provocatively: "If you were with someone new and then they told you on, say, your third dinner together, that they had herpes, would you see them again?"

"Hmm, I don't know," Hannah replies. "I think a lot of people who have herpes don't even know it, so the fact that they told you probably means they're responsible enough to get checked, and they know how to take care of it and everything. In a weird way you may be less likely to get it from them than from someone who never mentions herpes at all."

"I think I could do it if I saw myself marrying them," Mercedes says, "because then I wouldn't have to worry about getting it and giving it to someone else. We could just get married, be in love, and be happy together, and grow old with each other, and with herpes." Mimmo looks at Teta but she just shrugs and examines her nails.

"I'm going to say hello up at the other house," says Morgane getting up.

"Where exactly is this other house we've heard so much about? Can we come?" asks Mercedes.

"*Mais non!* It would not be right, turning up with lots of strangers..."

"Orran's there," volunteers Hannah.

"He knows them... it's owned by a group of collectors."

"Well then Wim should at least go up and meet them, if only to show them his work," says Mercedes.

"No. I don't want to. Let's keep things simple," says Wim with a brooding look. Wim has never been short of money so he has never needed collectors to buy his work. He had had his first exhibition at the age of forty-two, and then it was only because it pleased him, not out of necessity. He had never gone to art school. Instead he had travelled around the world on a motorbike with a succession of girls on the back. He didn't like other artists, never tried to explain his work, and didn't listen when Morgane did so on his behalf. She had introduced Wim to Orran, who had become very excited about his work when he found out that he was from one of the wealthiest families in Belgium, with a long history of supporting contemporary art. Wim's solo show of lewd watercolours had cemented a nice relationship with Mr. Dierickx senior, who was happy to see his middle-aged son finally doing something. He was now a major client, practically keeping the New York branch afloat.

"Somebody told me there are three types of collectors," says Hannah. "You have something called a 'completist', who wants one of everything. Then you have those who just want the best of something in a certain category. Then you have collecting by type, say frog ornaments or things with frogs on them. He said the last category is mostly women and the other kinds are usually men. What type are your collectors up at the other place Morgane?"

"They are the second. *Bonne nuit ma puce*." Morgane kisses Hannah's head maternally, puts on her embroidered shawl and leaves.

"That food was braw." says Sophie.

"Halal meat is really cruel." states Teta from behind her sunglasses. No-one listens, but she has lived in Los

Angeles long enough to know that much conversation is not listened to. It's done for the pleasure of talking, which means you can say whatever you want.

"Would you like to come for a walk by the beach?" Mimmo asks Hannah. He is like a bear round a honeypot.

* * *

Most people find Mimmo's appearance off-putting, if not positively terrifying. Not Hannah; she thinks he is the coolest guy she has ever met. He wears black, even in the heat, which the setting of the sun now has brought little relief from. He wears sunglasses and his moustache is dyed black to hide the grey. The next day Hannah will get a shiver when she sees Dupont et Dupond in a *Tintin* comic. He has had a very primitive hair transplant that looks like a black toilet brush poking straight up from his skull. They walk to the nearest beach, where families are enjoying themselves as the last of the sun's rays dance on the speedboats in the bay.

"What's that strange rock out there? Is it a lighthouse?" The flaming west outlines a black rock.

"Strombolicchio; little dead volcano."

"How big is it? I can't tell from here."

"Who knows, big as a mansion? Size is very important isn't it..."

Hannah looks blank. "Oh... was that supposed to be sexual?"

"No. If it was sexual I would have ended it with 'bowchickabowwow'."

She laughs and strokes his hand. She feels complacent joy, here on this stark island for the first and only time in her life.

Shooting Diary
Chapter 4

"Do you have any kids' books?" Hannah asks the sales-woman in the island's only bookshop.

"Do I have sex? Well…"

"No, do you have any kid's books?" Hannah repeats patiently.

"Kids? Yes. I've got one who's twenty-four and one who's nineteen. I know they're not really kids, but they still seem like it to me…"

"I said 'do you have any kids' books?'"

"Oh! Sorry! Yes, just there by the entrance," she gestures.

"Why do you want kids' books?" asks Orran.

"For a girl in the sanatorium by the beach that I got talking with this morning. She likes picture books, so I'm going to find her one. Dr. Davda won't let her leave the grounds. You know the reason Mimmo isn't dead is because of that sanatorium. Last winter he decided to have a New Year swim and got overwhelmed by the waves. The hospital is open all year round and he was spotted by a doctor. He was pulled out and resuscitated. Apparently he had been dead for ten minutes. But it was beautiful, he said, the colours, the feeling of the sea lapping against his face, the tranquillity."

"So drowning's quite a nice way to die?" They browse the shelves filled mostly with discarded holiday paperbacks in Italian. Through the window Hannah can see Mimmo talking on his mobile phone. She peeks at him over a copy of *L'isola del dottor Moreau.*

"Excuse me," Orran is touched lightly on the arm by the sales-woman. "Did I hear you mention crime?"

He stares at her blankly. "I beg your pardon?"

"I thought I heard you mention crime." Orran looks at her with disbelief. Inwardly panicking, he reviews in his mind everything he has said since entering the bookshop.

"It's just that the crime section used to be where you're looking now but it's just been moved to the other corner." Orran shrugs as she turns and walks away.

"I think she's really deaf, that woman," Hannah says as she studies her book.

Mercedes, who had been waiting outside smoking in the rain with Mimmo, wanders in. She flicks through a fat paperback and sighs. "People don't want good books nowadays," the words roll off her tongue automatically. "I can't read any more of those year-old copies of *Grazia* at the beach-house."

"Look, here's a copy of *Kidnapped,*" offers Hannah.

"I don't want to read Stevenson again. Does it always rain here? What kind of place is this? I had expected there to be more things to buy..."

They had awoken on their second day on Stromboli to a freak occurrence: clouds and a thin shower making the island dull and humid. It accentuated the barrenness of the landscape, with its black lava and scrubby gorse bushes. So both the orgy and the filming had been rained off. With the cancellation of their first day of shooting

Wim, Morgane and Sophie had made the most of things by setting off, under hastily found waterproof parasols, to scout for appropriate locations instead.

Orran gives Hannah a big bright smile, interested in what she has picked up. "Did you find something?"

"I think I'll give her this," she answers, waving the Wells paperback. "It's not a picture book, but she might identify with the theme. Wait! This is even better!" She pulls out a beaten up copy of *The Black Island* by Hergé from a haphazard pile. The comic is bought and bagged.

"Do you think Wim and the rest will be back yet?" Mercedes feels her wrist for a watch that isn't there.

"I'll go and see. I'm heading back to do some writing anyway. I need to work on my blog," says Orran.

"Tell them I've gone for an ice-cream. It's so hot and damp. There's no *air.* And Orran, give that darling stray kitten by the cactus on the road home a kiss from me."

They file out of the bookshop. Without interrupting his phone conversation Mimmo gives Hannah a surreptitious squeeze as she passes. Mercedes hooks her arm into Hannah's and leans in conspiratorially:

"Hannah Hazeldonk you have to learn to say no to those aggressive Italian men."

"Do I really?"

"No, I'm just kidding."

"I support chest hair."

"Good for you."

Mercedes turns into the café next to the bookshop while Hannah heads for the beach. She sees the girl through the chain-link fence as she turns off the path. The hospital's recreation ground stretches down to the beach and is deserted except for her. The girl is loitering by its perimeter in the rain, a wan figure in Chinese pyjamas, her hair plastered to her head. Hannah slips the plastic bag under the fence. The girl smiles when she peeks inside. She then adopts a supercilious expression: "Look! I treat my books like I treat people! Look! I rip the pages and bend the corners!" Hannah realises the girl is in a sanatorium for good reason.

"Do you like your doctors?"

"No. They tell me what to do all the time."

"Just because someone is wearing a white coat doesn't mean you have to do what they say. Ask them if they've heard of something called *The Milgram Experiment*."

She saunters back to the beach-house along the low road; the island has two, a high one along which the majority of businesses are clustered, and a low one by the coast. The rain has emptied the beaches, as if they have been evacuated before an eruption. She bows her head and thinks and walks.

At first it looks like no-one is home when she arrives back because the beach-house's large living room is empty of people, and contains nothing but equipment and Wim's drawings. She slowly climbs the stairs to the first floor. On passing Wim and Mercedes' bedroom she hears a noise that rouses her suspicion, and doesn't think twice about putting her eye to the keyhole. Orran is cramming what looks like bank documents into a calf-skin folder. She sees a Belgian passport and a bank card fall to the floor. She tiptoes to her bedroom down the corridor, more excited than worried by what she has seen. She finds Orran's pretty-man sparkle dubious because she is consciously developing her natural mistrust of:

1. authority.
2. charisma.

This is why she likes Mimmo so much. He is genuinely horrific. And anyway nice girls like bad boys, even though they know they are all the same. If Orran was doing something deceitful maybe it was time for some table-turning. Quite how she would do that she was not sure, she'd have to think about it. Right now, though, she needs to take a nap. The drop in atmospheric pressure has made her drowsy.

* * *

By late afternoon the clouds had dispersed, and now the evening air is pleasant and refreshing. Hannah is hanging around the kitchen, eying Morgane suspiciously as she spoons pasta into Wim's outstretched serving bowl. *I didn't come all this way for pasta and candles!* Her parents like to listen to opera while eating spaghetti in their big dining room overlooking the Cogels-Osylei in Antwerp.

She had hoped on this trip to shake off all that bourgeois small-mindedness and transform herself into a video vixen.

And here was Wim and Morgane acting as if they were a hale and hearty married couple. It made her notice the age gap between the two sets of guests in the house: Wim, Morgane and Sophie on one side as recorders and directors: and her, Mercedes and Teta on the other as the subjects to be filmed. Orran was somewhere in between age- and status-wise. *La donna è mobile* lollops along on the stereo, while Mercedes, Teta and Orran drink watermelon juice on the terrace. They are looking at the sketches he made of them once the sun had come out. He and Teta had sat and talked for hours while he made drawings of her looking pensive and frail. She loves them, it is the real her.

Hannah is relieved that Sirhan has been given the night off. He's a great cook, of course, but there is something about him that makes her feel uncomfortably self-conscious. She wonders if he even knows what they are up to here…

"Dinner will be literally two minutes."

They start to assemble. There are only six of them tonight because Sophie has gone to find a wifi connection. The air carries the smell of jasmine and rosemary from the giant bushes that line the path leading down to their secluded beach-house; there is no backlighting here, the rocks around the terrace are dark and teaming with lizards and ants. Plates are carried out to the terrace and candles are lit. Just as they are sitting down, a knock is heard at the front door.

"*Buonasera ragazze, ragazzi…* I'm just picking up some extra supplies from the big fridge. *Buon appetito!* Smells really good. No Sirhan tonight?"

"How are your dogs Chiara?" enquires Hannah.

"Very good. Just the bulldog of this Russian diplomat staying up at the villa needs some eardrops."

"What about all your strays?" asks Mercedes.

"Ah same. We're doing what we can."

"You know sometimes poor families with children that aren't taught well don't know how to treat animals. I wish there was something that could be done about them. You know it's not fair on the animals if they get placed into a bad home like that. If they don't have enough money to take care of their children, how are they going to take care of an animal? And they don't even treat their children right?"

"Ah yes…?" Chiara replies with a look of puzzled concern. Everyone else ignores the speech.

"Are you heading up to the villa now, Chiara?" Orran asks, looking at the plate of spaghetti in front of him with indecision.

"*Si si*, for the dog."

"May I join you?"

Chiara shrugs. "Sure. Oh, by the way, Mimmo will come over a bit later to check the leaky shower for you Morgane. OK, bye bye."

Orran makes some excuses, grabs his canvas bag of art materials and is out the door with Chiara in a blink.

"Did you get your cats from a shelter Morgane?" asks Mercedes.

"No, I bought them from a breeder."

"Why does she keep her stuff here?" Wim inquires of no-one in particular.

"Can we do something about that music?" Hannah asks through a mouth-full of pasta. "It's the third time the cd has repeated." She gets up and turns the volume down.

"She has to order medicine in bulk from the mainland and Mimmo lets her keep whatever can't fit in the shelter fridge here I suppose," says Morgane.

"*Lekker*, Morgane."

"*La meilleure sauce du monde, c'est la faim, ma cheri.* It's been a long day." Morgane smiles at Wim, her teeth stained grey from the red wine.

"Do we say that in Dutch?" Wim asked Mercedes, clasping her hand. Wim and Mercedes always look good together because they are both so remarkably tall, towering over the others, even sitting down.

"Uh huh, '*honger is de beste saus*'."

Teta silently slips off to her room; she has said and

eaten very little and wants to have a shower and get changed again. When dinner is coming to a close Wim stands up and wanders inside to contemplate his work, already thinking about tomorrow's filming. Hannah and Mercedes finish tidying up.

"What color is your aura Merc?" Hannah asks her cousin.

"Em, I think my aura has black and white stripes."

"Vertical or horizontal?"

" Horizontal. No, vertical."

"Is that because horizontal stripes make your aura look fat?"

"Yeah." She stretches and yawns. "I suppose I should go and practice for tomorrow…"

* * *

The location scouting earlier in the day revealed a suitable spot: an old burnt-out Fiat 500, hidden from view by high grass, off the winding dirt track that leads to the Observatory. Early the next morning, while it is still relatively cool, Wim surveys the scene and leafs through the folio of sketches he has brought. Here is one of Hannah and Mercedes entwined in a rickshaw that could be realized perfectly, transposed to the destroyed car. Morgane asks: "What are you imagining, Wim?"

"We can have Hannah and Mercedes in the white socks and geisha make-up. But let's use Teta as well. She's being paid by the day, after all. Seems like a waste…"

"It's not good constraining yourself with practicalities," muses Morgane, lost in a reverie. "Go with the flow… with what feels right. Maybe Teta can be spying on them… Eros and Psyche…"

The equipment, including a set of soft box lights that run on a heavy battery, is being carried up the steep track by Sophie, while Hannah, Teta and Mercedes get themselves ready on a picnic blanket nearby. Mercedes opens her professional make-up box, with its removable layers of cream and powder and other tools of the trade set out in rows. She is close enough that her breath disturbs the hair on Hannah's upper lip, and her nostrils whistle as she paints in eyebrows with great concentration. Teta is delicately applying vermillion lipstick to her nipples according to directions on a laser copied sheet of paper with photos and colour samples that Morgane has prepared as part of her art direction.

And then, just when everything is almost ready for the shoot to begin, it is announced that filming has to be postponed yet again. A special part of the microphone attachment has been left behind and Sophie will have to take the next Aliscafi to Panarea to get a new one. They cannot film without sound, because of the poems Mercedes is supposed to recite. There is some frustrated discussion, but it dissolves quickly into acceptance. Perhaps everyone is a bit more nervous than they care to admit about getting started on the cinematic masterwork.

The girls put their clothes on and file back to the house to remove their painted masks and get down to the serious business of sunbathing. "I'm going for a swim." Hannah packs her factor fifty sunscreen and towel and leaves. Mercedes and Teta lay themselves side by side on the terrace. Healthy young blondes in generic white bikinis: they look like a lazy imitation of a nineteen-thirties propaganda newsreel. If Wim had less of an *idèe fixe* he would have spotted this and created the film that Leni Reifenstahl never made for Mussolini. Sirhan, again at their service, sweeps the black sand that is forever accumulating on the terrace and in the house, averting his gaze discreetly from the women.

"May I draw you? To take your mind off things, dude." Orran asks Wim, who is milling around aimlessly, with nowhere to channel his frustrated creative zeal.

"No. I'm going to do some sketching myself." He walks past him to gaze again at his drawings.

"I'm going to the other villa, would you like to come?" Morgane asks Orran.

* * *

A small stocky man wheels a racing bike with bulging side panniers down the path to the beach-house. He checks the number on the house against a sheet of paper with spidery handwriting. He leans the bike on a weather-beaten cactus plant and holds his hand up to shield his eyes so that he can see into the house, which is shrouded in darkness. As he lifts his arm we see his sleeve ride up, there is a tan line, pale above, red and freckled below. He has been cycling for several weeks. He rings the bell and the door is answered by Sirhan, who indicates to Mercedes that they have a visitor, and who in turn hauls herself off the lounger. The newcomer explains that he is an old friend of Sophie's from Glasgow. She gave him this address and said there was a back yard where he could pitch his tent for a few nights, and a shower he could use.

"Sure, go ahead." Mercedes heads back to the terrace and her magazine. He follows her warily, wondering how many other bikini-clad Amazons there might be there.

"What's your name?"

"Callum. Callum Lavendar."

At dinner that night, prepared by Sirhan with mountains of fresh herbs over everything, the group accept Callum as a kind of stand-in for Sophie, and they ask him the same questions about Glasgow—a city none of them have every visited—that they had already asked her. Did people there really eat fried chocolate bars? Then they reminisce about themselves: Wim's opening in New York; the crazy party in Knokke last summer, when Hannah had to be carried home because of her low alcohol tolerance. Callum is self-contained and his presence is neither enjoyed nor resented. It's quiet in the house, Orran has been gone all day and Hannah had only come back briefly to eat before heading off to secretly meet Mimmo. The others sit around talking while Mercedes picks at her hair.

When Orran arrives back at the beach-house in the middle of the night he does not see Callum sleeping under a dark blue sheet on the couch. He shrugs off his V-neck tanktop. Callum awakens but lies still. He can hear Orran breathing quickly, as if he has been running. The garment hits Callum on the head as Orran tosses it aimlessly at the couch. Callum holds his breath while Orran gets a bottle of mineral water from the fridge and climbs the stairs. Once he is gone Callum lets out a volley of discreet sneezes.

Magical Realism

The study door opened with a soft kick. John Ramsay rematerialized, steady and careful in his socks, carrying a tray with caffetiere, cups and Italian biscuits, copies of the script under one arm. "… that's a cornu… A kind of Roman trumpet… it was lying around in the house we stayed in… scouting locations," John said, rolling his eyes in mock embarrassment and giving the door a little shove to close it. He had noticed Stuart squinting at the large framed photograph of a naked young woman balancing on a low wall miming theatrically as if blowing on a long curled brass instrument. Because of the sunlight behind, in the image she was more or less just a silhouette against a metallic seascape, and an odd little rocky tower of an island in the hazy background. You could just about make out the whites of her eyes. Stuart had taken off his shoes while John Ramsay was out of the room, guessing that this was the custom of the house.

"We took a lot of silly pictures of ourselves when we went to check out the locations. Actually a lot of them are really good. Full of ideas. I just really liked that one of Chloe. I think of it as a single image mood board, embodies the feel of the role. Like, a bit wrong? Like someone on the edge of something! There's loads more in the files…" John set down the tray on a low table and started arranging binders and copies of scripts.

"Like that sidekick girl in 'Dr. Phibes'!" Stuart said, trying to sound knowledgeable. "Actually… ahem, Vulnavia has a sousaphone in that movie… if you mean the final scenes…"

Stuart stopped listening to whatever John was going on about and flashed on an image in his head of those Florida A&M 100 guys he saw on American TV the year before. With, it turned out, and according to this new information, their sousaphones. They were like little hyperactive acrobats. He'd certainly never seen marching bands do that before, a hundred guys in day-glo Quality Street outfits racing around a sports stadium in perfect synchronisation, playing brass band versions of Ke$ha. And also, the memorable part, something to do with a story about death by hazing, the only reason the clip was on the news anyway. He wondered if British soldiers do those kinds of things, he still had half an eye on the Army. But—remembering—wait a minute, the Florida guys were only university students. Not even soldiers. Everything comes back to prison, he thought… that's something that needs changing.

He didn't know anything about drawing storyboards but had been urged by one of his mentors—the one who worked in TV—to give it a go, see if he could *help* with this project. He needed another push, which he had agreed about absolutely, and it had been made clear that most of all he needed to show that he could stick at something. Self-discipline was not one of his strengths, he just needed to look at his weight at the moment to be reminded of that. Maybe here he could begin to show a new spirit of determination. His parents hadn't sounded convinced at the idea—even after Stuart had been careful to rearrange the story to make it sound like a real job, a job that he'd been approached to take. In his gravest tones, Dad had stressed that if Stuart really had wanted to work in film and TV, he'd already be doing it by now. But in the end he'd agreed to keep giving him money until something better turned up, which was just as well because there would be no question of being paid for this. They didn't even bother to call this sort of thing an internship. It was 'Experience'. Anything to keep him off benefits! Which of course, he had been very much on—secretly—for years. With breaks in claims due to his very short term in prison. But perhaps this could be a stroke of luck.

Stuart had been to art college and, therefore, could draw. He was aware that storyboards existed etc, of course but couldn't remember looking at one closely. If he thought about it he would think he must have seen them on making-of documentaries but hadn't paid special attention. They were a bit like comic strips? He had brought a small folio of drawings, mainly stuff from art school days plus a few recent sketches of friends and some unresolved attempts at comic book artwork. But, of course, he certainly hadn't made any effort to really find out about it, do research. As ever, he decided to just turn up, see what somebody wanted him to do and take it from there. Just like the first day of working at Boots or Cineworld.

And now they were sitting facing each other around a low glass table sipping little melamine cups of coffee. Stuart placed his folio on the edge of the table and fiddled with his headband, tidying stray strands of his long dark hair. He'd started to accessorize like this when he put one on for a joke at a party and everyone had remarked how much he looked like Sergio Ramos.

John Ramsay picked up a script, handed it to Stuart and started leafing through his copy, stopping at one of the pages indicated with green marker tape. Stuart turned his copy round the right way. On the cover in double spaced capitals was

PAX GELATO

BY JOHN RAMSAY

"Its the scenes on the island that I'm most in need of your help, any help, visualizing," and he began to explain all about how he'd come to this point: he was forty-one and had directed a lot of music videos and three short films of his own—Facade Retention, Chips & Pins and something called Slimfast which he'd made for kids TV; he had been Director of Photography on dozens of film, television and ad productions; It was his work as DP on the successful British romantic comedy Note To Self that had allowed him to finance the development of another short film which, for the first time, he had also developed the script. The script had been seen by Christine Dupont at Canal+ and she had been sufficiently impressed to commission the production, for broadcast later in the year. With possibly a theatrical release. His partner, Baptiste—also with a solid CV of camerawork—would be DP on this production.

"Inspired by real events. I'd read about a girl who was drunk at the end of a night out and randomly killed some guy on the way home—she used her shoes as the weapon, it was *very* violent—and fled to Italy before being arrested eventually. No-one knows why she did it. In our film, we're changing the names and the locations… and adding a bit of humour. Its a black comedy. Sort of *noir* but contemporary... nods to Out Of The Past and Morvern Callar…

"Can I use the bathroom, please?" said Stuart.

Stuart didn't need to urinate and he often used the excuse of going to the toilet as an 'out' to buy a small space of time for himself in particular situations. As usual, he was standing in front of the toilet as if peeing. Maybe just in case someone could detect what was going on in the room. His mind was completely blank. Sometimes he struggled to detect any sign of a subconscious working away beneath his surface. His friend Simon always joked that he'd had his subconscious murdered years ago when he realised it wasn't any use to him. Stuart wondered where his was. Maybe he'd also accidentally murdered *that* in his sleep?

He took a moment to take in the mother-in-law's-tongue plant and the collection of Indian tiles standing on a small shelf behind the toilet. A pile of Sight and Sound's on the floor. The bath looked nice and clean. He checked his hair and let the tap in the sink run for a minute, glancing through a magazine left lying on a chair. He decided he liked the shells being used as soap dishes and pocketed the smaller one before returning to the study.

John Ramsay was aiming a remote at the sound dock, Coexist by The xx, very soft, barely audible. He rubbed his hands together energetically and continued, "So—yes—the story is that Marie, my protagonist, flees to an island in the Mediterranean and attaches herself to a group of rich people who, of course, have no idea of her recent past. They're shooting an arty-fashion porn film. They hang out for a week or so and then during a break in filming have a druggy orgy which goes badly wrong —one of the actress-models gets murdered. The murder gets blamed on an immigrant and the film ends with Marie leaving for another, similar island." Stuart was flicking the pages of the script, stopping here and there.

"There are some quite complicated scenes on location... parties, night shoots at the beach, filming at the edge of a volcano... which is at 1000 metres, let me tell you... its sort of one of the characters really. I'll need to have it all broken down into quite detailed shot-by-shot sequences so we can have everything planned, equipment-wise before we get there."

"Do you have images of the locations? It would be very useful..." said Stuart.

"Oh yeah, in the file... here, help yourself," John Ramsay produced an ipad, opened the file marked 'LOCATIONS' and passed it over to Stuart. "I'll email these to you, the whole lot."

John carried on, stressing the value he placed on the storyboard artists' role in collaborating with the director—under his supervision—to bring the vision succinctly to the screen. If there was any part of the process or the mechanics of filmmaking that Stuart wasn't familiar with, then John or Baptiste would be happy to fill him in. It was important that she would be involved with the storyboarding because she was the one with overall responsibility for the technical side of the shoot. Whatever Baptiste said about the possible set-ups for the shooting would be gospel. And there would be no need for the drawings to look particularly polished for presentational purposes because the production was already green-lit.

"As you know Hitchcock was especially careful in planning his scenes. Baz Luhrmann also, of course!" John added, "Danny Boyle movies are like watching a storyboard unfold in front of your eyes, don't you think?"

"Very much." said Stuart, cheered that John Ramsay seemed to be assuming they shared some reference points. While John had been saying all this, Stuart was clicking through the files of location pictures, exhaustive details from many angles of interiors and building exteriors. Also, a lot of images of the girl from the framed photograph in various outfits and different lighting situations. She had clothes mostly, although one set contained the sequence with the cornu. There were more shots of her clowning around, prowling like a cat, striking acrobatic poses or thoughtfully sucking a pen while looking at a notebook.

Storyboarding must, Stuart thought, be one of the many job titles in the film-making set up that's unnecessary. How can John Ramsay not know how he's going to shoot a scene? How can drawing pictures of what it could look like in theory help? It must be something to do with the projection of confidence and overall sense of composure. In his mind, he settled on: to *not* have storyboards would maybe seem too amateur hour.

"We're so lucky to have Chloe for this. I saw her in the German adaptation of Wetlands on Arte two years ago. She gave such a huge performance, very intense, beautiful —obviously—and would clearly be going stratospheric. But she was being very careful and wanted to finish her degree at Oxford, so kind of slipped from view a bit. Smart girl. Marie is her first role since officially coming back to acting..."

John's mobile murmured, making distant trebly

sounds of gunfire and screaming, probably downloaded from a game. He cursed under his breath and made a vigorous just-a-minute sign with his finger before beginning what sounded like an important conversation about casting, disappearing out of earshot. Stuart stood up and wandered around the room. He shuffled through some of the bits and pieces, papers and pictures scattered on the table. There was an embroidered military badge of some kind in bright rainbow colours with a wolf and eagles. He looked at a flyer in Italian with hand written English translations beneath the bulletin points, saying: *"1. The repeal of abortion law, 2. A social policy that encourages population growth and the traditional family. 3. Opposition to immigration and the humane repatriation of recent immigrants to Italy. 4. The fight against the Mafia, the banning of Freemasonry and all secret societies, together with exit from NATO and removal from the U.S. sphere of influence. 5. The fight against usury and writing off of public debt, as well as the abolition of capitalism..."* And on and on like this.

Although it was a sunny morning, a large cheese plant at the window acted like a screen against the daylight, casting gloomy shadows all around the room. Two of the walls were entirely covered by sturdy shelves holding hundreds of books, mainly mid-range paperbacks, travel literature, a lot of monographs about famous film directors and artists. Leaning against the books here and there were framed photos of friends and family with —prominently placed—a few photographs of John Ramsay dating from about fifteen years before showing him with bleached surfer hair, German army vest, combat trousers, holding camera equipment in varying locations, peering into viewfinders with rain forest in the background or perched high on a crane in moorland somewhere in the north.

He noticed behind a group of these photos a collection of erotic art books, Taschen stuff, Black Ladies, The Big Penis Book, The Big Book of Breasts, Erotica Universalis. He paused at Bic's Milica!, leafing the pages quickly and watching the familiar story flicker by, the glossy bulldozer demolishing the mosque, the leisure centre occupied by the commander for his HQ, the sex slaves, the reunion of Milica and her child, the escape by boat. Replacing it to the shelf, he speed scanned the others Vin Rude, Sumo, Gustav Klimt's Erotic Sketchbook, Erich von Gotha's Feuerblume, Guido Argentini's Silvereye, Shunga, Neü Sex, David Hamilton's Dreams of a Young Girl and his absolute classic masterpiece Maiko Minami. He made a mental note to steal this if left alone in this flat.

"I have always failed to "get" the big deal over Sasha Grey," John Ramsay was standing right behind Stuart, who hadn't heard him come back from his phone call. "She was hopeless in 'The Girlfriend Experience.' Unintentionally hilarious. A rare mistake by Sodeberg? He's an underrated genius, by the way!" He slid the book out from the shelf and started flicking briskly through the pages. "What happens when narcissism and incompetence get together and make a photo album? You get Sasha Grey's "Neü Sex". Baptiste sent it to me when she was working in the States. A joke, of course!" He fixed Stuart in the eye, like he was waiting for a response.

Talking about pornography always made Stuart feel very uneasy, almost ill. It set him off badly. He had clearly defined ideas about this, the proper boundaries for discussion. He felt that pornography should and must exist, but only in secret—in an ideal world it would be freely available but never mentioned. If people still thought and acted as if it was wrong there wouldn't be so many problems in the world. Although, his experience of prison had left him convinced that life inside would be far more peaceful if pornography was freely available there.

"I noticed you looking at my copy of 'Ordeal by Roses," said John, "Mishima, and all that... *stuff* is not my cup of tea... just to make that perfectly clear! It's those Eikoh Horsoe photographs that interested me. Bic's a genius. He actually does story board work himself from time to time..."

"This is a great flat. Have you lived here for long?" Stuart said.

"Ten years. We bought it when my Father died for almost nothing, when nobody was living round here. But now... have you seen the rest of it? Let me show you the kitchen—its got a wonderful view of the park," he gestured Stuart towards the hallway.

The glossy black fridge reminded Stuart of the bulldozer in Bic's adult comic. It also made him think about something he'd heard about it being important nowadays to know that organic cafes favour black fridges. Next to the fridge the kitchen's casement windows came down to floor level, with the treetops of the City Park spreading out beyond. "What a terrific view," said Stuart, "I've never seen it from up here. You must see even more in the winter, without the leaves. You can see the Stadium over there!"

"Oh yeah, sure. Although I'm almost never here in the daytime. A day like today is very unusual. A luxury. So that's what this place looks like in daylight!" said John, "by the way, that was Christine from Canal+ on the phone. We're going to be able to use the Muse track I wanted for the arrival scene at the jetty!"

"Yes?"

Seeing that Stuart seemed under whelmed he felt he had to explain further, "It's normally completely out of the question to use existing songs or pieces of music for this type of production. But with the Canal+ people behind it..."

"Is that you in the copy of Fantastic Man?... in the bathroom?" said Stuart.

"Oh no! I mean, yes! Very embarrassing—it was all because of the video I directed for Van Hoogstraten. *That* song? That was us, and the magazine wanted to do a thing about new British 'talent'. The rest is history... between ourselves, making videos can be *very* boring but the money is well worth it if you can get it done quickly enough."

"Yeah, that video was everywhere last year," said Stuart.

"Tell me about it. Wish I'd got paid per view! Oh, I must show you the 'director's cut' version of the video... everyone on the crew got in on the act," John was searching for files on his phone. "Ah! Here it is... now—you know how in the actual version the giant basketball is being pushed up the hill by those really tall basketball players?..."

As John Ramsay was saying this he smiled and glanced briefly at Stuart to make sure he could see the phone's screen. Stuart, seeing John looking at him in a slightly encouraging sideways manner felt this was confirmation. John Ramsay was signalling to him. He though that maybe he had been signalling to him earlier when they were looking at John's books. The remarks during those Japanese photographs looked more like a playful, diversionary tactic now. They could have been some sort of test.

But at the same time, he knew that sometimes some people just had one of 'those kinds of faces', which made things very complicated. He felt at least ninety per cent certain that the sign was now being transmitted, loud and clear, and it would be foolish not to act on this immediately. Foolish and unwise, given the situation which was after all a kind of informal job interview, but a job interview nonetheless. And a job that could be very important for Stuart. Who knows where this could take me, he had thought earlier. So time to make a guess, which wouldn't be so much of a guess.

He leaned towards John, simultaneously sliding his arm around John's back to pull him closer. He half closed his eyes and swivelled his head to angle his mouth in line with John's. This will put the dot on the 'i', thought Stuart.

John immediately flinched backwards, cracking the back of his head sharply against the edge of a kitchen unit. He looked dazed for a couple of seconds, then doubled up as the pain spread and rubbed his head furiously. His face was angry and dark red. He looked at Stuart as if he was completely mad.

"What the fuck are you playing at?"

Stuart, panicking, instinctively jerked forward to rub the back of John's head, desperate to make amends for misreading the signs. John tried to swerve away from Stuart but, because he was now crouching, fell over hurting his knee and letting out a loud yell of pain. Blood was now trickling from a nosebleed, as if everything else wasn't enough. The blood made Stuart even more panicky.

"Get out! Get out!" shouted John Ramsay, gurgling and spitting through the blood dripping into his mouth. Kneeling, he took a moment to let a long elastic string of blood drop to the kitchen floor and closed his eyes tight for a few seconds before starting to shout at Stuart to get out again. Stuart, frozen in panic, and watching John writhing on the floor, snapped out of his horrified gaze and pounced on John to at least try to stop his shouting. He had heard some muffled sounds of kids laughing and squealing in the upstairs flat earlier on and John's shouting must have been at least as loud. If he was very unlucky they would be heard through the walls or the floor or the ceiling. Holding John with no more than a moderate force from behind his head and then his throat, he held his other hand over John's mouth to stop the noise. John struggled in fits and bursts but with all of Stuart's bulk bearing down on top of him he couldn't wrestle himself free. Although he was shaking with the effort, Stuart thought abstractly for a minute or two: he really wanted to be involved in this film, it was a great opportunity and if things went well with the storyboards he might even get brought along for the shoot on the island. If the film itself was successful, it could very well lead to other jobs, maybe in Canal+ or the BBC. He even pictured himself briefly in the kinds of locations in John's framed photographs.

When he refocused back in the present, John Ramsay had slipped into unconsciousness or something, and Stuart was out of breath. His arms and legs were hurting and he was sweating. Blood from John's nose was all over his sleeves and front. John might have hurt his head badly when he hit it on the unit, so Stuart dragged him by his arms to the bathroom, dragging along a cream rug and a book that got stuck beneath John as he slid through the hallway. He thought he'd better do something with water on John's head. He had seen a movie where one of the characters has a fit and his friends help him by covering him with ice in a bathtub. This was different, but at least in the bathtub he could clean John up without making more of a mess of the kitchen.

He hauled John into the bathtub, scattering magazines and toiletries. He wished for a second that it was all the other way around and it was John who had made the move on him, Stuart, and then it would be John Ramsay who would have to tidy everything up, make the effort to make amends. Another silly fantasy! Never mind, he said to himself, let's keep to the job in hand.

It took him about ten minutes to get John undressed and he went back to the kitchen to catch his breath, it had been really hard work. He noticed that John had filtered water in the fridge and he helped himself to a glass, wiping his brow with the back of his sleeve to avoid the bloody area on the front.

John Ramsay had turned blue. Sad and blue, thought Stuart, and also as if he was thinking deeply about something. His eyes had dark rings around them and he looked like he shouldn't be disturbed. His face had taken on a serious, far-off look, which Stuart had noticed before when studying people sleeping. As he busied himself wiping the blood from John's nose and mouth he remembered the life drawing models at evening classes. Sometimes they would fall asleep if they were in reclining poses and, if they were old enough, their faces would, when completely relaxed, all have the same solemn expression. Once he had videoed himself asleep to see what expression *he* had when he was unconscious.

Stuart breathed in and out deeply, stretched his arms, tried to touch his toes. He rehearsed a karate chop move he'd learned. Reaching around John's body, he lifted him out of the bath and back on to the rug. Using the rug this time as a sled he dragged John to the study and hauled him on to the sofa before collapsing on the armchair beside the window, beginning to sweat again from the effort. He looked over at John, slumped on his side on the sofa with one of his arms trapped beneath his body and decided he ought to pose him differently. He got up and watched him from various vantage points in the room before deciding to make him lie on the couch with his feet up on the end arm rest and his hands behind his head, 'lounging'. He walked back through to the kitchen to turn on the gas.

Then he found himself looking again at the book shelves. Martin Amis, William Boyd, Ian McEwan, Zadie Smith, Bruce Chatwin. He picked out a big Phaidon encyclopaedia about art and tried to look at some pictures before realizing he wasn't interested. A thicker, taller white book caught his eye and he swivelled his head to read the spine: 'David Hockney: A Drawing Retrospective'.

He slid the book out of the shelf and sat beside John, turning the pages slowly. A cutting from an old newspaper with a review of the book and a birthday message marked a page in the middle. The review spoke of the artists' 'enduring career… brightly coloured paintings imbued with breezy decadence, world travel, and theatrical gestures', but Stuart had stopped at a sober line drawing of a sleeping man on a sofa, his arms resting behind his head. Feeling relaxed now, he lit a cigarette, picked up a nice pen and some paper from the table, squinted at John Ramsay and began to draw.

Shooting Diary
Chapter 5

"Is anyone home?" Chiara knocks at the door. Callum jumps up off the sofa where he has been napping. He makes a non-descript noise to indicate his presence there.

"Oh. Who are you?"

"A friend of Sophie's. Everyone is out, filming."

"Ah, OK. I just came to check my fridge—the shelter was broken into yesterday, so I want to make sure everything is OK here. Yes, the padlock is still there, no trouble. Really strange. You have a nice time on Stromboli!" She leaves and Callum flops back to the couch.

Sophie had returned from Panarea where she had picked up what she needed from a contact of Mimmo's. She had been badly stung on the lip by a wasp that had landed in her drink as she waited for the ferry back that morning.

"Always use a straw! Always!" Callum had warned her when they had spoken on the phone that morning. He always held the mobile away from his ear when speaking to her because she shouted so much. She and Callum had lived together in Glasgow before she moved to Berlin to look for work; now she had a young family and travelled a lot working on various film projects. Callum would often time his epic cycling tours of continental Europe to coincide with a visit to whatever location Sophie was based at, to get a bed and a shower en route.

He examines the backs of his hands, where the skin was cracked from a combination of sun, sweat and wind, checks his supply of anti-histamines and then tries to doze. The heat is really getting to him. After everyone disappeared off to the shooting location he had moved his blow-up mattress close to the water's edge to get a breeze. But then, because it was impossible to sleep, he had slipped into the water and stayed there for a long time. When he eventually got out, the heat was still so intense that after no more than two or three minutes he was already bathed in perspiration again.

* * *

With Sophie's return, filming has resumed. Equipment and white-socked geishas are in place up at the burnt-out car. It is a day of unrelenting sun and stillness. Sophie lines up the shot; the rusty old Fiat with its front seats ripped out and dumped in front of it is in the centre. Seen through Sophie's viewfinder, the car is framed by fico d'India cacti, with unwholesome prickly pears still attached, and looming behind it a huge, ropey ficus tropicales. The mood is effectively exotic. The three girls wear nothing but frilly ankle socks; Orran is in charge of a large stock of them because according to Wim's stipulation they have to be pristine throughout the shoot. They have the primitive geisha make-up applied by Mercedes, which, in combination with their fair hair, looks incongruous, but Wim is adamant that the scene should correspond exactly with his drawings.

Mercedes has learnt lines of Wim's poetry beforehand, and her job here is to recite them dreamily as she and the other girls slither around in the grass in front of the car. This is to develop slowly, like a kind of ritual, into a scene involving all three girls on the car seats. Orran stands behind Sophie, clutching some of Wim's drawings and the stash of socks. Ostensibly his role is to have these things at the ready when they are needed, but he is really there to offer moral support. He is still smoking the Brazilian cigarettes he had bought in the airport when he had to smuggle a figurine to Rio in his luggage for Greengrove last month. The warning images on the cigarette packaging are the most hysterical he had ever seen. *When did it become normal to see erectile dysfunction, rotting teeth and lungs displayed on everyday objects?* A transgressive exhibition aimed at a very precise audience, and with a specific response in mind. Maybe he should mention this on his blog—it would look really interesting next to the stuff the Russian diplomat had told him on Thursday evening. But now Morgane is calling for fresh socks, so he snaps out of his daydream and fishes some out of the plastic bag.

Mercedes physically dominates Teta and Hannah, who are both very slim in build. Though he has photographed Mercedes and her cousin together many times, Wim has never requested them to actually have sex, perform together, until now. It is easy to tell they feel uncomfortable with it, but they are trying their best, determined to please him. Hannah moans orgasmically then brightly queries "Are we done yet?" The poses into which they contort themselves are meant to show their bodies to their best advantage to the camera. The relationship is to be with Wim and the viewers, not with each other. It looks forced.

Orran takes Wim aside and they talk quietly. In the meantime, Teta, as the professional, has decided to take things into her own hands. She is bored with all the shilly-shallying, and the poetry and the writhing, and frankly doesn't care for the analogy between a tongue licking a vagina and a brush on canvas. So while he is distracted she dispenses with Wim's direction and instead forces the girls' bodies into the more graphic positions she knows so well as a mainstream porn star. The bourgeois Flemish girls suddenly find themselves out of their depth and start giggling nervously. For a moment it feels as if the mood has changed to one of real possibility, but somehow this too fails to get going. How can they create an atmosphere of voluptuousness if they are forever stopping to change their socks, which they have to do because of the dust that is being thrown up by their writhings on the filthy upholstery?

After five hours of false starts, sock changes and make-up retouches, Wim shouts: "Cut! It's not working. Let's call it a day and pack up." He strides off down the mountainside leaving everyone else hanging mid-shot.

Teta's hostility to everyone is kept under strict control, but she is running out of patience with this group of amateurs. She has performed in the most abject group sex at least three times a week for the last two years. She is, at this moment, one of the most recognizable young starlets of the adult film industry, signed exclusively with a top production company. She thinks of herself as an athlete rather than any kind of artist, and she is trying to be absolutely the best at what she does. She does not take drugs and she practices yoga and Pilates specifically prescribed for porn actresses for two hours of every day. She thinks Wim's project is grandiloquent bullshit.

* * *

The whole household has heard Wim and Mercedes fighting in their bedroom, but have chosen to ignore it; no-one discusses the afternoon of frustrated fantasy. Callum made excuses to Sophie about wanting to sail round to the other side of the island and visit Ginostra, but the truth is he could not stand the atmosphere on the group's return, not in this terrible heat. Orran, equally anxious to escape from the oppressisveness of the place, has disappeared to the villa on the hillside, but not before he had persuaded Sirhan to leave the house on an errand so he could pick the padlock of the fridge in his room and extract some interesting-looking pills. These he has secretly given to Wim with a conspiratorial nod. Now Morgane, Teta, Sophie, Wim, Mercedes and Hannah are eating dinner in silence. Everyone is drinking more than usual to compensate for their discomposure. Sirhan, back now from his short trip, goes about serving and cleaning unobtrusively in the background.

"I cut myself on a rusty spike," whines Mercedes rubbing her upper arm.

"Well my face is fucking sunburned and I've got heatstroke!" Hannah snaps.

"You have to put up with it—it's your job." Teta is the only one who looks happy and animated. The moment of control she had experienced in the afternoon has made her come to life, as if the familiarity of her vocation has made her step out from behind a curtain.

"It's not my job," says Mercedes. "It may be yours but it's not mine. I wasn't brought up like that."

"What *is* your job? Or do you get your money at the bank of Mum and Dad like everyone else here?"

"What's your problem, Teta?" asks Hannah. She is in a terrible mood, picking at the skin that is already flaking off her nose.

"This is rubbish. Your film is not sexy and you have no idea." Teta throws down her napkin. Everyone falls silent; she begins to talk with great passion. She explains to them as best she can in her basic English that pornography works to a special tempo. If you don't obey the rules you will never produce anything erotic. You can't ignore, for example, the importance of the little opening scenarios that draw the viewer into the narrative.

"Huh? Those tacky stories about pizza delivery boys or school teachers?" asks Wim with a sneer. "This is art. What I'm doing is much more edgy. I know what I want to see and what turns me on."

"Do you want us to enjoy ourselves while you are filming?"

"Yes, if it looks good to me."

"But you don't notice when someone is starting to lose control, the way they should, because you are fixed on your stupid accessories. Poems are not sexy. And neither are the socks and make-up, Morgane."

"That's your opinion…" says Morgane, clearly put out at having her authority in matters of erotica questioned.

Teta explains that clichéd scenarios are essential to porno films because otherwise they just look like violence. So the scenario can even be rape, but it should be exaggerated and hyperbolic so it is not mistaken for the real thing. What they were doing today was too vague; Wim and Morgane do not understand the mechanics of the genre. She has an instinctive sense of what works in films like this, although she has never tried to articulate it before. Her agent had said her talent had arisen from all the horse-riding she had done as a child, all the non-verbal communication with large muscular beasts. But she knew that was only part of it, and not the most important part. On set, she had always loved lingering after a shoot to hear the crew discuss how the scene had gone. In a roundabout way, and always dressed up as bravado, they had somehow got to the fundamentals: the structure. One day she will be a director herself, and then she will recreate the incident, nine years ago, that had fused sexuality and danger together in her psyche to such great and lucrative effect.

"I know you have some kind of drugs Wim—I saw Orran give you a packet of something from Sirhan's room. Everyone; let's drink vodka and take some pills and I will teach you about how adult films work." She says this in a way that is both commanding and seductive. No-one can believe the difference in her temperament, now that she is in her natural domain. Wim pulls out a small cardboard box from his pocket.

"What exactly are those pills Wim?" asks Morgane dubiously.

"I don't know. Orran told me this afternoon that he had spotted them in the fridge and thought they might… help."

"That fridge is always padlocked," says Sophie with a furrowed brow.

"Yes, it's strange. He says they are some kind of animal aphrodisiac. Thought we could use some to spice up the filming."

Teta snatches the package and starts popping out small white lozenges into her palm. She presents two to each person in turn with such an air of authority that they cannot refuse.

To Sophie she says with a smile: "Just one for you. You are going to have to film everything."

Sirhan, pretending not to see what they are doing, continues slowly loading the dishwasher and fussing with wine glasses.

"Mercedes, you speak Italian don't you? Tell the boy to take two of these pills then run and buy us some vodka from the bodega," Teta orders. Mercedes holds the pills up to Sirhan's face and instructs him to do what he is told. He does so; he is apprehensive, but he does it all the same, then leaves the house. While they wait for his return Teta uncorks a wine bottle and tells stories about her experiences as a porn star. She does a slow, expert striptease. The pills are working; everyone starts to tingle. They start drinking more and chuckling. Mercedes and Wim start stroking each other's bare arms and Sophie dips into the salon to fetch her camera, her eyes bright and wide.

By the time Sirhan returns Teta has pushed Wim onto the table, climbed on top of him and removed his t-shirt. She tells Mercedes to take her clothes off and climb onto his face. Sophie and Hannah stand back to admire the unfolding scene. Hannah catches Sirhan's anxious but decidedly stoned expression. She weaves over to him and takes his hand. "Don't be scared" she whispers, her face close to his. She pushes him against the fridge and feels an erection despite his worried eyes.

Sophie reaches for her camera…

The next thing we see is that she is filming Teta slapping Mercedes hard across the face as she has sex with Wim on the table. The vodka bottles are already empty and the room is in disarray. Wim is staring over Mercedes shoulders at a mono-print of him having sex with Mercedes. In the drawing she is holding something in her hand, and then he remembers. He clambers off her and goes upstairs, returning unsteadily with Mercedes' handbag. She has rolled off the table and is encircling Sirhan and Hannah, kissing Hannah over Sirhan's shoulder while feeling her way into the side slits of his djellaba. Wim pulls out something shiny from the bag.

"What's that?" asks Teta, who is looking over Sophie's shoulder at Hannah, Sirhan and Mercedes in the viewfinder.

"It's for Mercedes: she can't orgasm without her mirror. When she was a child she had lunch at her grandmother's house every day. She sat in a room and ate on her own in front of a mirror."

"Gimme that!" Mercedes pleads. Teta snatches it from him. "She can't come until I say so!" She looks at Wim with a mixture of anger and jubilation. "Strip out the intelligence! Know your market! Ahhh, finally! Some fun!"

"Well it's not really about that…" Wim mumbles incoherently, looking serious but still swaying. Teta strides up to him and grabs his face.

"This is what we need isn't it?" She laughs at him. He nods beatifically, completely in the thrall of this demonic orange pixie.

"Sophie, hold the camera straight. We need something more…" Teta looks around. Sirhan has his eyes screwed up tight, but is fondling Hannah's breasts, as if by keeping his eyes shut he does not have to acknowledge what he is doing. Teta drags him and Hannah into the centre of the room and one by one forces them both to swig from a wine bottle.

She whispers in Sirhan's ear: "You will never win you know." He neither hears nor understands her, his eyes are rolling back into his head. Teta guides his hands around Hannah's throat and squeezes.

Sophie looks at the scene through the camera. Sirhan's fingers around Hannah's neck in the half-light look wonderful because she is using a digital filter for high contrast.

Teta marches around the room. She orders Wim and Morgane to fuck, which they do, with glazed expressions, on the floor. She screams at Sirhan to strangle Hannah. He is crying. Teta grabs his hands and locks them around Hannah's neck even tighter. Hannah is almost unconscious; her tiny frame has no defence against the heat stroke, the drugs and the alcohol. Sirhan, drunk for the first time in his life, is still gripping Hannah's throat, and the glee in Teta's face makes him grit his teeth and squeeze even harder. Sophie comes closer, Morgane watches from the floor, everyone is complicit in this tableaux.

At this point Hannah blacks out, but only momentarily, and by the time she comes round again adrenalin kicks in and the spell is broken. Sirhan is looking at her in horror. She staggers to her feet and blearily takes in the scene. She sees Wim pounding away at Teta while Sophie films it; Mercedes masturbating while staring gravely at her own reflection in the hand mirror; Morgane smoking a cigarette and looking on blankly, wearing only her big red bra. In the shadows her face looks like that of a gorilla's—an intelligent and friendly gorilla, but a gorilla all the same.

Hannah tumbles out of the villa, coughing violently. It is the middle of the night and she is lurching through the unlit streets, up past the bookshop and bodega, through the empty town square and up the hill to Mimmo at the villa. She has to stop on the way to vomit, but only manages a dry retch. Suddenly, she realises she does not want to see Mimmo after all. She has changed her mind about him, found him lacking the other night when they had lay in the bushes after she spied on Orran.

* * *

Orran had just started to enjoy a cigarette in the grounds by the main gate of the villa when he notices a figure scrabbling and sobbing on the dirt track outside. He peers through the gate and recognizes with disbelief that it is Hannah. He presses a button and the gates swing open slowly. She stumbles to a halt when she realizes there is someone there and that it is Orran. He blocks her entrance to the villa, but instead of turning back she continues on the path to the no-mans land of the volcano. Seeing her gasping for breath with eyes the size of saucers he knows Wim has taken his advice and given her the canine love potion.

He recognizes a window of opportunity here, and as she takes off from him at a heavy run he decides to follow her. But first he stashes his canvas tote bag in a bush, removing from a side compartment something that he places in his pocket. There is only one path up the volcano, much of it winding in zigzags. They are not fast, this tag team, but they are quietly concentrated, and their progress is steady. He is surprised she does not try to take off in another more oblique direction, but she sticks to the path that is clearly visible in the moonlight. After a while they both in their own way zone out of reality, forgetting what they are doing as they fall into the rhythm of running. But she is so dizzy that he soon catches up with her. He grabs her t-shirt, wrenching it so hard it rips down the middle, its Egyptian motif torn in two. She struggles to free herself, panting that she knows he is evil and he will never catch her. But he not only does catch her, but punches her in the stomach to make sure she knows it. As she doubles over, heaving for breath, he grabs her left breast with a clunch (a cross between a clutch and scrunch), and twists it maliciously. She screams, but a kick to her already bruised stomach sends her sprawling unconscious beneath the stars. He stands over her, panting, his sandy hair falling over his forehead and the sweat stinging his eyes. He rests for a few minutes, regaining his breath, and looking at the spectacular view. Then removes from his pocket a vial of clear liquid and a package containing a syringe. He knows that poison is typically a woman's murder weapon but in the circumstances it seemed like the best option.

It now occurs to him that the best way of disposing of her body is by dropping it into the volcano, so he heaves her over his shoulders and staggers further up the hillside, a combination of endorphins and madness guiding him in the dark. But it is too difficult and he gives up, just dumping her by the path instead. For dramatic effect he pulls off the remains of her clothes and pockets the scrunched-up ball of jersey cotton. He decides not to go back to Klem's bed, but to the beach-house, curious to know how Hannah had got into the state she was in, and what had driven her to the momentous moment when she had crossed his path.

Shooting Diary
Chapter 6

Mercedes and Teta do not materialise that morning, and everyone else is preparing for the scheduled shoot, despite their hangovers. All are somnambulant. The house is a mess and Sirhan is gone. The last anyone had seen of him was when he ran into his room in tears the night before, locking the door behind him. He may still be there. Hannah had disappeared at some point as well, when they were too distracted to notice. Those up and about were not sure who had seen her last. Maybe the sleeping girls knew something, but everyone was still too drunk to care.

Morgane is leaving on the six o'clock ferry to the mainland; she has to get back to Paris because she is curating the next show at the Palais de Tokyo.

Filming today is exclusively of her. She is to stand on the rocks and read a text she and Wim wrote together when they first became friends ten years before. Wim had written to her in 2003 care of the art magazine she was editing at the time. He had sent her unsolicited love letters and poems, collaged into photo books along with his first attempts at erotic sketches. His letters expounded on how her face and body had been an access ramp onto the road to discovery in own sexual journey.

In the mid-1970s Morgane had been used as a model by her artist mother, who made faux Victorian photographs, rather like Lewis Carroll's of Alice Liddell. She was only thirteen and the images made her a cult figure on the Paris social scene. She posed for famous photographers and painters, and had bit parts in several mainstream films, always in the role of a precocious poppet. She came to symbolize something of the prelapsarian licentiousness of Paris at the time.

But it was in the 1990s that Wim had seen her in a film, and realised that images of her were used on things like gig posters and record covers. He started collecting works depicting her; he wanted to be a collector like his father, but not of contemporary art. He wanted his libido to direct his acquisitions: she was a cult, not a prize. Then he discovered that the well-respected art critic and curator Morgane D'angleterre and his fantasy girl were one and the same person, and that even though she was now a stout fifty-year-old, sensuality was still her stock in trade. She had the same jet-black bobbed hairstyle. For her part, she had cultivated a friendship with him, the gangly millionaire with money to spend on things like research trips to Thailand. She had encouraged his drawings and photography, discussing them in the private language they had developed together. When his show had opened at Greengrove he presumed people would be shocked, or at best it would have a niche perverse following. He had been rather puzzled when it had been accepted so readily by the audience. He had not noticed that tastes had changed around him.

Teta reminds Wim of the young Morgane; Teta is to be her stand-in because Morgane has become too old and ugly to appear in the film. He knows that the sublimated sexual energy between him and Morgane can be expressed through the text that she is now rehearsing, but sleeping with her the night before had changed things, killed something, and he has completely lost interest in the shoot. Right now he would just like to go back to bed.

Her scene is long and she has to read from a print-out. She stands with her back to a clear horizon, a small round shape against the sky, intoning in her most expressive, breathy French. Orran stays quiet, wondering if anyone will tell him what exactly it was about last night that makes Wim seem so cold and detached from the shoot.

The filming drags on all morning, and at about lunchtime Mercedes and Teta emerge from their bedrooms.

"So do I have to make my own coffee since Sirhan is not here?" Teta asks petulantly.

Mercedes chugs from a bottle of mineral water and points at the group on the rocks in the near distance. "They're filming on the coast out there. That would be even worse than that car. Think of the cuts and bruises you'd get. Have you seen Hannah?"

"No, she must be with them."

"I can't see her. Look at Morgane out there. I'm sure the reason she's such a mess is because she never had any kids. Oh, whatever. I'm going to go back to bed."

Morgane has finished her scene and is ready to leave. After goading Wim into doing this film she too has now lost interest, and wants to get home to her work and her cats. A golf-buggy taxi picks her up directly from the beach, her bag already packed, and Wim and Orran accompany her to the port. Orran is to join her soon to assist her in her Palais de Tokyo organisation because she will exhibit several of the Chinese painters he represents. As she waves to her boys (that is how she thinks of them) from the departing ferry, she notices that the air has changed: something is missing. And then she realizes she no longer has the odor of bitter almonds under her nose. She will die of breast cancer within a year.

* * *

At the precise moment when Morgane was watching the scene at the port recede from her, Hannah's body was being discovered by a group of tourists scaling the volcano. Tours depart from the main square at five and the trek is timed for the most spectacular view of the sundown and lava eruptions. It had been too dangerous the day before and a hike had been canceled, so this one was fully booked.

Her body was a long way up the mountainside, and it wasn't until the hikers had been walking for an hour after passing the last civilized landmark—an overgrown eighteenth-century graveyard—that they had spotted it. In a panic they fled back down the hill en masse and as soon as phone reception was available the tour guide called the local police. There was no way up the mountain except on foot, so a helicopter had to be organized, and it was midnight by the time a tent had been erected over her body and halogen lights trained on her corpse. The volcano announced the horror to the island populace with a particularly dramatic series of booms.

She was naked, and the exposure to the prolonged intensity of the sunlight had turned her pale skin a livid red. (One of the policemen who had lifted her body to place it in the body bag had got to see just how white the unexposed skin had remained, apart from some cuts and bruises, probably sustained on the way up through the lava rubble. On one side the skin was so pale it was almost green; on the other it was the colour of chopped liver. The man later told his wife that it had reminded him of something he had read in a book about the battle of Stalingrad. In the living winter hell of the kessel, cadavers had been kept warm next to an open fire so that the lice stayed on corpses and did not infest the soldiers. If the guard fell asleep or forgot to turn them regularly in the extreme cold, one side would roast and blister while the other side froze. His wife said it sounded more like a victim from Nagasaki and would he please stop talking about it.) But this is what Hannah looked like now: her entire front was scorched while her back was as stiff as ice. What a contrast it made with the unblemished pale skin turning a delicate rosy pink in the afternoon sun or from repeated kissing, and that sweet freckled face that Wim found so essential for his autoerotic photos. Now her skin was as tight as a sausage and gas was making the corpse expand in the heat. She had been bitten all over by insects, so that if there had been any punctures in the skin, from say a hypodermic needle, they would have been impossible to detect. But despite all this, and the blisters, the strangle marks on her neck were perfectly visible.

She was identified right away as the funny little redhead who hung around the sanatorium and played tennis with the mad girl and the dyke doctors. The island is small and they knew where to look for her companions, and by early the next morning the police chief has called on Mimmo.

* * *

Wim and Sophie have left early to shoot prolonged scenes of natural landscape. Later they plan to hire a boat and record the lava rolling down the north-west escarpment, the impasse that separates Stromboli town from Ginostra, its counterpoint on the other side. They will also pick up Callum, who has been camping there.

Teta is in her room doing yoga when Mimmo and the police arrive. Mercedes and Orran are getting some morning sun before the relentless heat will drive them inside again. Orran answers the knock at the door. Mimmo translates for the police officers and everyone falls into stunned silence. Teta emerges and is informed of the death. She asks if she can have one of Orran's cigarettes, which she smokes intently, alone on the terrace, with short fast puffs. She then returns to the group and calmly tells the police that Hannah was murdered by the Iranian servant who came with the house. Both of them had disappeared two days ago.

"She wasn't with you, Mimmo..." says Mercedes looking vacantly out the window. Mimmo lifts his hands in a gesture of innocence.

"Do you have any photos of him?" asks the police officer.

"Of course I don't!" Teta snaps. Mimmo tells them he might have a photo, or rather his employee Massoud might. They try to contact Wim and Sophie but there is no reception. Orran offers to come to the police station. He thinks to himself *this house must be absolutely dripping with DNA after what seems to have happened on Friday night!*

More hunky Italian policemen arrive and look around the house, cramming themselves into Sirhan's tiny room and disrupting food packages stored there. The inhabitants are led out onto the terrace and the police cordon off the building with striped plastic ribbons.

Forensics arrive and start dusting for prints, while on the other side of town Sirhan is informed by Gustav Klem's Filipino maid what she has heard and he scales the fence of the villa, just like Hannah had done, and disappears into the vegetation.

Mercedes and Teta calmly make their drawings for the police. When they are done they go for a drink at the local bar, not wanting to wait around for news in a house full of upheaval.

Over a bottle of beer Mercedes asks: "Why did you say Sirhan did it, Teta?"

"Because he's a filthy Arab rapist," she replies calmly.

"What…?" Mercedes cannot process this. But before she can question her Teta asks: "So why aren't you sad that your little cousin is dead?"

"I am sad, but it is her punishment."

"Punishment for what?"

"You wouldn't understand. You're not spiritual."

"How do you know what I am? My family is Sufi."

"I thought if anything you would be Russian Orthodox?"

"No. I get accused of being Russian a lot, but I'm not. I'm from North Ossetia. Chechnya"

As Mercedes looks at her, a distant memory starts to stir of history classes back in Gstaad. But her thoughts breeze over the bat-squeak of recognition and return to the sanctimonious mumbo jumbo that usually fills her head.

But maybe now you, reader, are getting an inkling that you have seen Teta somewhere before, and not just on your laptop. Look at her closely because you *have* seen her before, wearing even less than she wears now, years before she started her professional career. You did see her on the internet, but in a digital reproduction of the cover of a newspaper called *Izvestia.* Remember? There was a scandal and the editor of the paper had to resign. She is twelve, semi-naked, terrified and wounded, with long brown hair, bendy childish limbs. She is clinging to a young man, who may be a Russian soldier but it does not look like it. Maybe he's just a Chechen like her. The image gratuitously fills the front of the newspaper. When the picture was published no-one knew if she was alive or dead. She had been part of a group of hostages, starved and terrified for three days. The Russian forces had tried to seize the school and capture the Seperatists who had killed her classmates with their incendiary rockets. The editor had had to resign because the image looked far too much like the kind of pornographic scenario she later came to excel at enacting.

Mercedes shakes her head, as if trying to explain something to a small child. "It's punishment for something Hannah did in a former life, don't you understand?"

"I'm glad I'm not busy with this kind of thinking like you."

"I think sometimes women want to be killed. It's all a mystery. Manifest destiny."

Even Teta's steely heart crumples at the sound of these words.

Not Going to Lie

Dear Baptiste,

Stromboli is amazing. We watched this great documentary last night—on the patio, projected onto hanging bed-sheets (!). Can't stop thinking about it. These apes are high in the forest canopy silhouetted against the sky. The crew must be running as fast as they can in the tropical heat with all their equipment to keep up with the men from the village, who look incredibly fit. Showers of leaves and twigs falling on them as the apes leap around among the branches—while the natives fire darts from their blowpipes. One of the apes becomes separated from the troop and gets hit by a dart as it attempts to jump to safety. All the men just seem to wait around discussing what size it's going to be… then it falls, paralyzed, crashing through the branches and vines to the forest floor. The men are all crouching round the ape, poking leaves up its nose and tying it to a pole to carry the thing back to the village. Everyone from the village is excited because they're going to eat the brain later on, and the presenter joins in too! I wonder what it feels like to eat a primate?? After we watched the film everyone went swimming in the sea with headband torches—it was pitch black, warm, scary but wonderful.

Question: have you seen or heard from Marie recently? Her career seems to have stalled—I wonder if she's the kind of person who might be good for my project?

What are your thoughts?

Have you heard anything about her, or what is she up to? Basically—is she still in UK or gone back to Paris? Hope you're well and your work is going good,

Very best regards,
John

About five years ago I told John about this guy I went out with at school who made fertilizer bombs from empty fire extinguishers. Just for fun of course. He knew he could get the fertilizer from garden centre shops in the suburbs and set it all up in an abandoned quarry outside the city. A little gang of us would drive out to lie around the edge of the quarry pit smoking hash and drinking vodka, waiting for these enormous explosions, which could take forty minutes to happen. It wasn't very exact, the sealed-in fertiliser granules had to reach the critical temperature by being roasted on a bonfire. We couldn't go anywhere near it once everything was set up, just had to wait it out until it went bang. And once, he used an old beer keg, which made such an incredible explosion. When we went down to the edge of the pool where the keg had been there was nothing left that was any bigger than a fifty pence piece. If anyone had been standing within a hundred feet they'd have been cut to tiny pieces. We never thought of that! We found a rabbit that had been caught in one of his fire extinguisher blasts and was completely shredded. John found all this really interesting, asking lots of questions about the guy and saying that he had to track him down and make one of his films about him. He used to pester me about it every time I'd see him, for ages. It was hard work to dissuade him and put him right off. I don't want to get in touch with these people! That's one of the reasons I'm not on facebook. I don't want people like them back in my life!

John talks in code. He sends coded signs like a lot of people I know, to be fair. Things he says often seem to have other meanings or subtle suggestions beyond, behind, beneath what appears to be the focus of the conversation. The usual way would be for him to say something very straight forward, on the face of it, but which masks a hidden suggestion inside. He might say something along the lines of "I saw this painting you would really like..." and you would be unsure whether he likes the painting himself, or thinks its average and wants to imply that he thinks you are average. Or he might say something really affirmative about a piece of work or a film he's seen and then I'll get the feeling that he wants to know what you think about it. Or even just whether you are open to being manoeuvred into agreement with him. It's even possible that the feeling of unease, in itself, is the goal. I can spend days weighing up discussions we've had, searching for the principle subtexts. I wonder if he learned to do this or if it just comes naturally? But maybe I'm over-thinking? I don't know if he's really clever enough to plan this. Maybe it happens by instinct.

You have to be careful of what you say or it can end up in his work. I once said something about wishing I could still think there were people behind cinema screens, and a robotic autotune singing voiceover in one of his videos duly announced the same words. I don't mind about things like that.

He's very influential. So many students are making little versions of his work. John shoots everything on 16mm now, much more expensive, but a lot more to do with 'cinema', materialist. He used to make videos from found footage but now concentrates on these films which shift between interviews with people talking about themselves on camera, following them around and collaging the material together. Interviews are presented deliberately out of sync, subjects appear suddenly upside down, interspersed with apparently random imagery. A view of a retail car park might appear with exposed negative flare bursts and then it might cut to a tracking shot of stuff lying around on a mantelpiece or close ups of a plasma screen showing clips from 'Game of Thrones'. If I had to describe them to my parents I'd say they're sort of like documentaries but not really. I like them.

And now John is back in touch and wants me to help him find someone else for another of his projects. It looks like he's doing really well now, has shows all the time in Europe and the US and he's in a lot of actual film festivals.

Marie is a model who was around about a year ago —a friend of a friend. I think she's from Lebanon. In reply to the email I said that, yes I had wondered what she was doing and that I'd heard she'd had some kind of meltdown and gained weight. But then again I'd seen her at a show in London back in September during LFW and she looked really happy, but I couldn't tell much at first because she was across a room. When we talked she seemed positive about everything and was in fact signed with Ford+ and I was under the impression she was getting a lot of work in that division. We actually had a short conversation where she said her weight gain was somewhat inevitable since her teen metabolism had completely gone at a certain age, and that it would be impossible to maintain that skinny frame in a healthy way. I didn't add in the reply that I personally thought this sounded lazy and unmotivated to me. If everyone thought that way, there wouldn't be any models over eighteen years, only teenagers with good genetics who retire as soon as they hit their twenties.

I asked him if he wanted me to put her in touch, he replied within ten minutes:

Dear Baptiste,

Thanks for the message—it must be a difficult situation for her, I had actually heard something drastic might have happened, but whatever it is and whatever's going on in her life right now I really have a feeling she could be a very apt person to collaborate with in this project. Maybe this could also be a positive way for her to get back in touch with people? People often want to come back to their friends after taking time out. It would be so good to have someone embedded within the work who is / has been involved in the fashion industry. Here's a short outline about the project:

"Unlawful Assembly"

One enters the community of one's equals not by being equal to them but only by being like them. There is no way of being counted one of them without reflecting their own image: an equal is someone who's image is that of an equal. Making a virtue of usefulness, playing the card of function, is merely to preserve one's dissimilarity. No redistribution of members, functions or bodies can transform unlike into like.

For the main part of my show in Cologne I'm making a film based around Jean-Luc Godard's 'British Sounds'. The original has six distinct sections of which I'm doing 'remakes' of three: the MG Midget auto workers on the assembly line at Abingdon, a newsreader quoting passages from Engels, and a naked young woman hesitating at the top of a staircase.

She needs to be someone who isn't an artist—won't necessarily be recognised as a known persona by the type of audience its safe to assume will see the show. It's really vital in fact that nobody knows who it is. If it could be someone with modelling experience that would be great, because she also needs to look amazing—which is why I immediately thought of Marie.

This villa at Stromboli has a staircase which would be perfect for this scene—I'm sure the people overseeing the project here would be fine with her coming out to stay for the filming.

I'm also filming elsewhere in Italy—in the Lamborghini plant at Sant'Agata Bolognese, which I just received permission for, and which is a very exciting prospect.

I've got someone who is working on finding an Italian newsreader to read the quotes.

Best regards, John

* * *

I met Marie in some place on Frith Street. I don't think she's going to walk at any shows again, or even wants to. Actually I'm sure. But she's still in London and says she's applying to do teaching of some kind, next academic year. I got the impression that it could be difficult to persuade her to take part in the video, but she gave me the OK to give John her email and she said she'd certainly think about it. She actually seemed pleased to have been considered for a role in John's work—it turned out she's entirely familiar with it and had seen it a few times at various exhibitions. And when I mentioned the trip to Italy of course seemed a lot more interested, so perhaps it wouldn't be so hard to get her to do it. I didn't have the nerve to mention she'd have to do the part without any clothes on, John could take care of that.

But before I got around to contacting John about it I got another message:

Dear Baptiste,

Hope all well with you—I hope you haven't had time to get in contact with Marie because the project has changed a bit since last week and now I don't need someone to do the role discussed before. But there's something else I hope you can help with.

I've been talking to some of the people who are also doing events here, watching a lot of Adam Curtis, and it seems like maybe the ideas for the work I was planning before might be problematic in the sense that the 1968 angle has possibly become exhausted and is too clumsy politically for me to credibly use as material—so I've decided to make a different work for the show in Germany, something that will more silently reference the Network. As someone here said, I'm using too large a net—I mustn't be catching dolphins when what I really need is tuna.

Do you know that guy Bic? I think he was on the MA course when you did it—he's maybe Croatian or Serbian. I think he still works at the University, maybe in the digital imaging department or something? I'd really like to interview him for a piece of work, about his life etc. He used to make those strange adult comic style drawings. If you can think of any way to get in touch with him I'd be really grateful—I've changed phones about fifty times since I last saw him and if I ever had his number its gone now. Let me know what you think.

I wish you would think about this. Will you do that for me?

Perhaps, it might spark new ideas for you also.

Everything else is cool here, there's some really great people and great work and everything,

Best,
John

I was annoyed for a few seconds, after having gone to the trouble of arranging to get hold of Marie, and now that was a waste of time. But when I saw him mention Bic's name I laughed to myself and thought it could be fun to get in touch with him again. I already see him from time to time at the University.

Everyone found Bic completely impenetrable at first, his accent was so difficult to understand, and he found us just as impossible. Also, his facial expressions seemed limited to nodding, blinking and very occasionally creasing up with laughter, which he would involuntarily try to mask by shielding his mouth with one hand. Then instantly returning to his default blankness, which would make everyone else laugh. He seemed fascinating at first because we knew that his family had been refugees from the war in Yugoslavia but no one had the nerve to ask what had happened over there. I can't remember if he was Croatian or Serbian or what. Someone there claimed to know it was all an act and that he was from Bedfordshire and was just hiding from the CSA. I'm not political so I didn't care either way.

His work was taken to be an ironic reference to adult-erotic graphic art but after a while it was clear that he was really only interested in this kind of work and there was no irony intended. He was impervious to theory or any kind of further reading and wrote his dissertation on other comic book artists he admired. Other than trying to get him to make on-canvas versions of his drawings, the staff kindly left him alone and he completed the course as quietly as he had begun.

I liked Bic. People often take the opportunity to yawn when I speak, or interrupt me to begin an alternative conversation with unrelated topics, but Bic always had good manners and would wait silently until I'd finished. He was fun in a minimalist deadpan way and had an impressively amateurish looking Partizan Belgrade tattoo on his chest, which he showed us one night when we were all trashed. It must have hurt.

* * *

Bic's buzzer is just an apartment number, no name in a small 1980's block of flats on a leafy hill in the south of the city. He shouted to me from the top floor banister as I climbed the stairs,

"Do you have any cigarettes?"

"Yes!"

"Good. I can't be bothered going out on my days off."

In the gloss green paintwork of a landing someone, a child by the look of it, had scraped 'THE OLD LADY IS A SLUT'. On the next landing in the same scraped handwriting it also said "BIC" followed by something in Cyrillic. At the top landing, I gave him a tiny friendly wave and he very slightly nodded his head, flickering his eyes toward the door to indicate I should go straight inside. Avoiding a lot of empty beer bottles neatly lined up and waiting to be taken downstairs, I stepped into the flat.

"A nice surprise," he said gravely, but with a slight smile in his eyes, "Haven't seen you for a while. How's everything? Still working at the University too?" I remembered how people used to say that when he smiles he looks like he might loose it at any second. I smiled back:

"Yeah, still doing a couple of days a week. Keeps me going."

"You want coffee? Tea?" he said, in an even lower tone.

"Coffee, please... if you're having it too,"

"Yeah, yeah, always..."

He took one of my cigarettes and left me at the entrance to his main work room / living space. He didn't hint whether he wanted me to follow him to the kitchen or make myself at home in this lounge, a long wide room with windows at both ends, and a frosted glass partition leading to the kitchen. The glass was frosted in funny vertical waves. I just went straight in and looked around respectfully, like I would at an exhibition.

"I will be five minutes," Bic called, from the kitchen. His accent was nothing like as heavy as it had been at art college, almost ordinary English.

The window out to the street had a small concrete balcony. A large glass-topped wooden desk sat in front with a laptop, a printer, drawing materials, papers, scattered on the surface, all kinds of stuff which must have been source material for something.

I looked out to the grey daylight beyond the balcony and across the street, at a derelict church without a roof. The plain ground-glass windows at the front were still intact above a wooden door protected by chained wrought ironwork gates, ornately rendered to resemble ivy branches. The gates form a shallow cage around the door. You could see down into the interior thick with weeds, rubbish and small trees. I saw a couple of cats carefully picking their way through the debris. One of them was standing on a statue that had fallen over. It looked like there must have been a fire, perhaps a long time ago, the walls looked as if they had been scorched, or it could have just been dirt. I continued my tour of the room.

He had some pictures neatly arranged on one wall: a large photograph of two competing black male sprinters, maybe from the London Olympics, one in focus, the other blurred, both with their faces hidden in total shadow; a film still showing a scene of Christ on the cross. In the white border at the bottom it said "Golgotha: directed by Julien Duvivier"; a careful line-drawing of a naked sleeping man on a sofa and finally, a framed original artwork which must have been Bic's own drawing, of a colossal ape enveloped in clouds of gas, overcome and on the point of collapse. The ape was crying out something in a Cyrillic speech bubble.

"He's saying 'No to the Accession of Serbia to the European Union'... I made this as a poster for political friends," Bic said, carrying a small tray.

"The gas is amazing... do you use an airbrush?"

"No... its just a simple trick. Normal brush"

Bic pulled a couple of chairs around the table and set down the coffee cups.

"You're still up at the University too, right? The digital imaging department?" I said.

"Oh yes, still fixing stupid problems of students. Always leaving everything to the last second! What's up? You said you have something you need?"

"Well, its not me really... its something for John Ramsay,"

"I can't believe he needs my technical assistance. He must have many assistants for this!"

"Its not technical... its more personal. Or, persona to be exact. John asked me to find out if you would be willing to take part in one his films."

Bic's eyes flickered wider, "Story boards?"

"No, no, its not technical at all. He wants to interview

you. You would be the subject of the film…" Bic's mobile started vibrating noisily on the glass table with the ring tone gradually increasing in volume, a recording of gunfire and children screaming, no doubt from GTA or something. He looked at the screen for a few seconds before answering and had a short, clipped conversation only answering no or yes to whatever a distant tinny female voice on the phone was saying. He held the pose at the end of the conversation for a few seconds, as if frozen, like he was thinking carefully about something.

While he had been speaking I glanced around more closely at the material on the desk. There was a cd by 'Ceca', described as turbo-folk on an inset sticker, the album called "What's That In Your Veins". I could also see scattered pictures of supermodels cut out from magazines, a light box, tracing paper, print-outs from military hardware catalogues, books about uniforms, and print-outs of screencaps from porn movies.

"I have to make a private call. Two minutes", he said, and opened a drawer under his desk to lift out a small black metal device with 'Safescan' written in white. It looked electrical, but I couldn't see what it was for. Grabbing another package or something, also from the drawer, he got up and took both items through to another room.

I imagined John's interest peaking to new levels, if he could see this scene. I took the opportunity to have a look at what Bic was working on, a series of drawings for one of his adult comics. As I leafed through them, I could see his style was precisely the same as it had been years before, when I first knew him on the MA. Very skilful, slick renderings of smoke and liquids, all the characters looking like models with ultra modern hair. I changed seats to be able to look at the pages properly.

Disgusting gratuitous sex and violence everywhere.

This story was clearly intended for publication somewhere. The cover mocked up and inked said 'MILICA!' in large, graffiti-style letters with drips and a frowning woman's face in high contrast, as if it was stencilled and sprayed on a rough brick wall. There was a small publisher's logo in the top right corner, some chains with a pair of disembodied lips. Judging by the cover page, it was going to be an adult-erotic story of a young woman caught up in a brutal civil war. Bic's name was modestly sized at the bottom of the cover page, in the same street style writing. I had a look at the following pages. The arrival of a paramilitary motorized unit at a small town by a river. The commander, handsome and dark with a pet albino wolf cub on a chain, alternately straining at its leash and pawing the commander. The men in the unit all have the same black military fatigues and berets with insignia of crowns, triple eagles and wolves surrounded by a rainbow coloured shield shape with the letters 'BPC' at the top. There was a real, slightly different embroidered badge lying on his desk among all the other stuff. I don't know why, but I grabbed the badge and stuffed it into my jacket pocket.

On another page, the unit huddled, saluted and quickly dispersed to begin destroying the town, firing missiles into houses and shops, setting fire to small factories. A glossy black armoured bulldozer demolished a mosque. They rounded up the men, shooting them or stabbing them to death, throwing their bodies into the rapids of the river below. Bic had the RATATATATATAT! gunfire words snaking across several frames, like in most war comics. One frame showed, in silhouette with deep red background, a man being raped before he got shot.

Next, the militia established a base in a local leisure centre. The men rounded up local women and have brought them to the leisure centre, which has a sign in Cyrilic. The women are all based on well known supermodels mainly, as usual traced from ads, but are all crying as they are separated and made to disrobe. The commander was shown taking off his clothes too. He looked exactly like John Ramsay, Bic had drawn his pale eyes perfectly. This put the dot on the 'i'. I made a note to self to mention this.

Then, a series of more loosely pencilled frames showing alarmingly violent sex scenes and warfare which must have been waiting to be finished. It looked like the focus of the story was Milica, the beautiful young woman of the story's title, caught up in a civil war and separated from her child. On the last page I saw she was reluctantly removing her headscarf to reveal shining platinum hair. Bic had given her an intrepid body-stance, wide-set, expressive eyes, thick brows and pouty lips. Perhaps the commander would become infatuated with her and help her, and so defy his ethnic-cleansing orders.

"I have to visit my friends in hospital," said Bic, returning to the room with his jacket on. "Been badly injured at their shop. Cash for gold place. He says the Russian guys beat them and smashed up their store because he won't agree to buy their second hand gold jewellery." Bic was shaking his head, but looked fundamentally unmoved.

"That's awful… do you know if they're ok?"

"Can't be too bad, if he can speak on the phone. This has happened before. I have to go. You'll have to leave too, sorry. Tell John to email me at work, although I'll tell you now: I don't want to appear on camera, I hate having my photo taken. Maybe he can get an actor to be me?"

"I'll give you John's email, and you can contact him if you feel like it, after you've thought it through. There might be a trip to Italy. He understands how it could seem odd. He said something about not wanting to catch endangered sea birds with the same line he's using for tuna, I think." I got up and looked around the room again. "I really like your drawings, especially the ape. When is the story going to be ready?"

"In a couple of months. Its just some work I'm doing for a company I do stuff for."

As I was unlocking my bike I thought, how straightforward everything is with Bic. I made another note to self, must get Bic to draw my portrait, with gas rising around me.

When I got home I found the badge from Bic's desk in my pocket and studied it for a few minutes. Inside of the shield-shape eagles and wolves stared at each other beneath the rainbow colours. I tried to picture the little factory somewhere in the Balkans with the contract to make these kinds of things. After dinner I wrapped it in tissue paper, sealed it in a strong envelope and mailed it to John.

Shooting Diary
Chapter 7

The police were happy to close the case quickly, bribing the Messina coroner into recording that Hannah had died from inhaling the naturally occurring poisonous gas emitted by the volcano while she was under the influence of alcohol and an unidentifiable drug. Since the fatal poisoning of several volcano-worshiping hippies who had decided to live in a camp at the summit, no-one was allowed to visit the top unaccompanied. Why she had climbed there not wearing a stitch in the middle of the night was put down to the strange things that teenage girls do, driven by the same insanity as the volcano-lovers, whose brains were warped by the natural phenomenon's power to entice the credulous into acts of folly. Perhaps Hannah, a sporty youngster, had scaled the mountain instinctively, compelled by its hypnotic pull. Maybe when she got to the top she had planned to hurl herself into what she imagined would be a gaping crater spewing lava. Instead she would have discovered that the volcano mouth was actually a vast undulating terrain, like the surface of Mercury or Venus, scattered with a multitude of oozing, hissing orifices. Confused and exhausted like Ingrid Bergman in the film, she must have lain down for a sleep from which she had never woken up.

There were no suspects. Sirhan was cleared, Mimmo was the chief of police's mate, and no lunatics had escaped from the hospital.

Wim, still unsatisfied with what he had done, had insisted that they keep working on the film, which was nowhere near sexy enough yet. But with Teta's input it would be, and Orran thought the tragedy would be great for viral marketing before its showing at the Basel Art Fair next year.

Mercedes now saw Wim's face as a circle with an X where the mouth and eyes should be. Sophie needed the money.

* * *

"Hi there! You catching the SNAV too?" Orran greets Callum on the gangplank.

"Yes, I'm going to try to make it to Matera today. I've only done about a thousand kilometres so far on this trip."

"You're Sophie's friend, aren't you? The cyclist... Lavender? I have a beautiful Colnago back in Brooklyn. You should see it. Well, enjoy your trip."

They part company and settle into seats on opposite sides of the lower deck on the morning ferry to Messina. Callum squints at the view and applies some eczema cream to his chapped hands. He forgets Orran and dozes off, the chug of the boat overriding the sensation of nausea induced by the smell emanating from the headrest, which reminds him of hamsters. The Sicilian coastline eventually comes into view through the salt-streaked windows. Callum thinks about the last few days. He is looking forward to getting back on the road, back to solitude. What can a cyclist do on such a small island? It was odd, though, that the Belgian girl had died like that. No one had seemed to really care, which was strange because he thought she had been quite sweet in a spoiled kind of way.

It was not quite true, that no-one cared. The little girl in the sanatorium had taped the pages of her comic book back together and wished Hannah would come to visit her again.

Callum knows that the man he can still vaguely make out in his peripheral vision is a liar and a conman, and he doesn't need to know why. He is convinced he is Hannah's killer. He recognises in him the same coldness that he himself feels towards people in general. But while he can understand why someone might kill in a rage, he can't figure out how anyone could commit murder if they were not driven by anger or panic. What if it was done for no reason at all, just on a whim? This, he can see now, is where they differ. Callum was selfish and lazy, but he had enough of a conscience to check any impulse to physical violence. But the question still nags at him: why had Orran killed her? He realises that he does actually want to know. He wants a closer look and he decides to investigate the matter; it would give him something to think about while on the road over the next few days.

Once they reach Sicily, the short ferry ride from Messina to the Italian mainland port of Villa San Giovani is much quieter; most travellers are heading further into the region. Callum and Orran stand together on the deck.

"This is a bit like the journey from Oban to Mull," Callum lies.

"I've never been to Scotland," Orran replies with a lie of his own.

"I see your sketchpad there. Did you get a lot of sketching done?"

"Oh this..." Orran looks down at the sketchpad poking out of his rucksack. "Yes, I did a lot. Actually have you seen a garbage can anywhere?" He spots one and saunters over to it, takes out the sketchpad, folds it in two and shoves it into the bin.

"But what about your drawings?"

"Don't need them anymore. They've served their purpose. When someone sits for their portrait they feel as if they are being appraised, but in a detached way, and they like it. I found that out when I was at art school and made some money on the side as a life-model. It's an extreme form of hiding in plain sight. You forget that people are looking at you. That's when I learned to stop talking to myself, which was a bad habit I had. I would blurt things out and find myself making all sorts of admissions without realising it. Bad idea!"

"But the drawings?"

"I'm not really an artist. I only do them as an ice-breaker. You meet someone well-known, or rich, and you ask to draw their portrait. So you get to sit and chat with them and they're flattered, especially if the sketch is complimentary. I used to keep them, thinking one day I'd do a show of all the interesting people I'd met through sketching them, but I think that idea has run its course."

The mainland is getting closer; the ferry's engine is shifting gear, slowing down.

"The thing is, people tell you things too, like at the beauty parlour. The Russian diplomat at Klem's villa told me some funny stories when I drew her on Tuesday.

And they seemed to chime with something Teta had told me about someone called Umarov, some kind of Sharia Emir. I don't know who this person is, but the story was so entertaining, I thought it would make an interesting article, and posted my thoughts on my blog. Teta really hates Muslims you know."

"Didn't the diplomat disappear?"

"Yes. Bizarre isn't it?" They gaze at the view.

"Was it with something from the dog shelter? Is that how you killed Hannah?" Callum asks with genuine curiosity and no judgment in his voice. Orran stares straight ahead at the coastline.

"But the other good thing about these psychiatrist couch sessions masquerading as life drawing is that I get to hear why normal people do what they do, why they get so upset about things. I think it's because I wasn't held as a child, I just don't have the feelings you are supposed to have. All these people with their codes of ethics, they just seem like suckers. It's good to have a stock of stories to make people feel sorry for you when you need them to. People will do anything for you if they feel sorry for you. I write them in a notebook." Orran turns to Callum and smiles. "And it's somehow nicer to take than to have, don't you agree?"

"Sometimes."

"You have to be a little bit smarter than everyone else, but not much. And it's nice to have nice books, buy nice things. My boss wants me to run a franchise for him in Dubai, which would be great because women don't seem to like me as much as they should. In Dubai I wouldn't have to deal with them would I? Hannah discovered I was fleecing Wim's father, she caught me with some documents. I know she saw me, and I couldn't run the risk of her mentioning it to anyone. You know, blah blah blah, the usual story. Jeeze! But it looks like I'm going to have to hide anyway. I've got a feeling I might have to keep my head down for a while. It doesn't look good, that diplomat disappearing like that. Anyway, yes, it's called Pentobarbital and it's what you put dogs down with. I heard her moaning about how she'd put on weight from all the pasta, and was fifty-one kilos so I knew how much I needed. How did you guess, by the way?"

"There was dog hair all over your jumper when you came home on Thursday night. I'm allergic to it."

"Really? Wow you are quite something."

They turn their back on the view and look at the cluster of tourists on the boat instead.

"Hey, are you into mnemonics Lavender?"

"I love mnemonics. Use them all the time."

"Can you believe I managed to *guess* Wim's pin number? 2504."

"I remember mine as 'The Tudor *Année Érotique*'."

"1569?"

"Exactly. So how did you guess Wim's?"

"He mentioned sulphuric acid just after I asked him if his cash card worked on the island. H_2SO_4 is it's chemical formula."

Callum had witnessed plenty of narcissism cozied together with incompetence on his little sojourn on Stromboli, but this was not Orran's problem. His was the combination of vanity and indiscretion brought together in a self-contained immoral unit. And he seemed suicidally talkative this afternoon.

"There I go again with my big mouth. You won't tell anyone will you? No-one need know of my life or my projects."

"Who would I tell...?"

"Good man. You're cool you know that? Here we are." The ferry bumps to a standstill and they part.

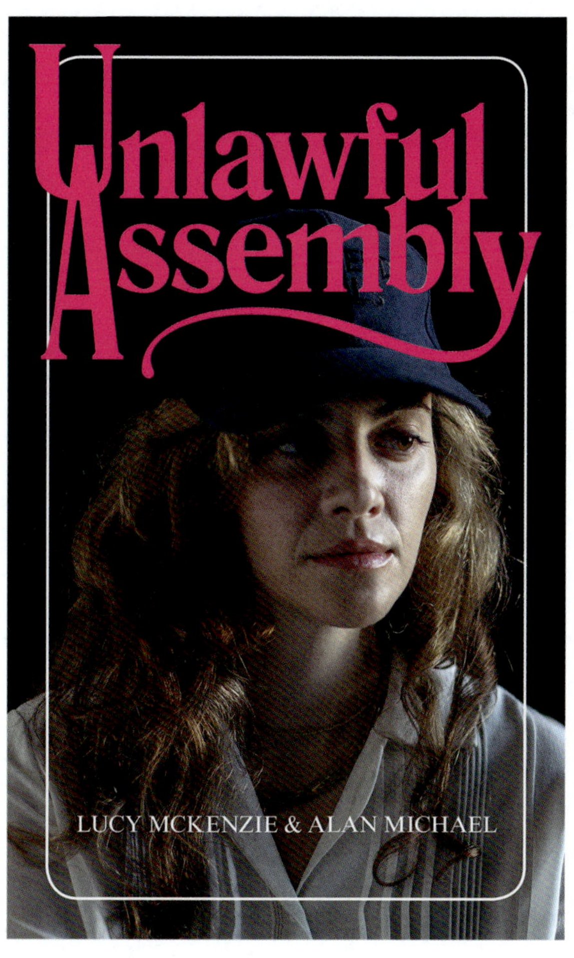
Unlawful
Assembly
LUCY MCKENZIE & ALAN MICHAEL

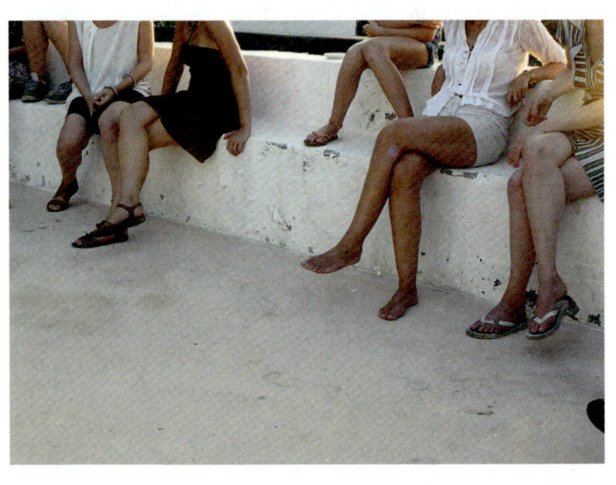

Lucy McKenzie
Stromboli 1, 2013, digital photograph
Courtesy the artist

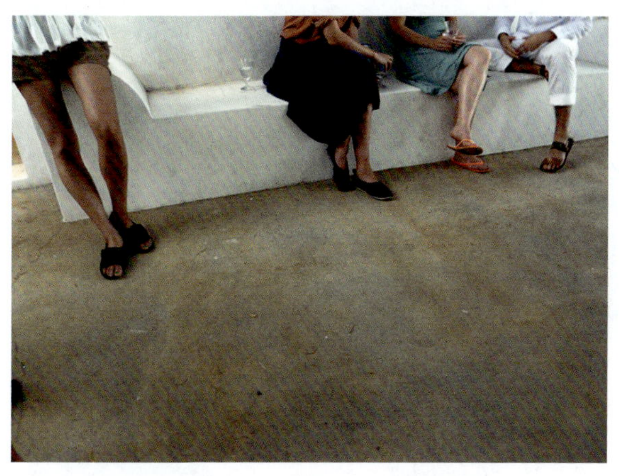

Lucy McKenzie
Stromboli 2, 2013, digital photograph
Courtesy the artist

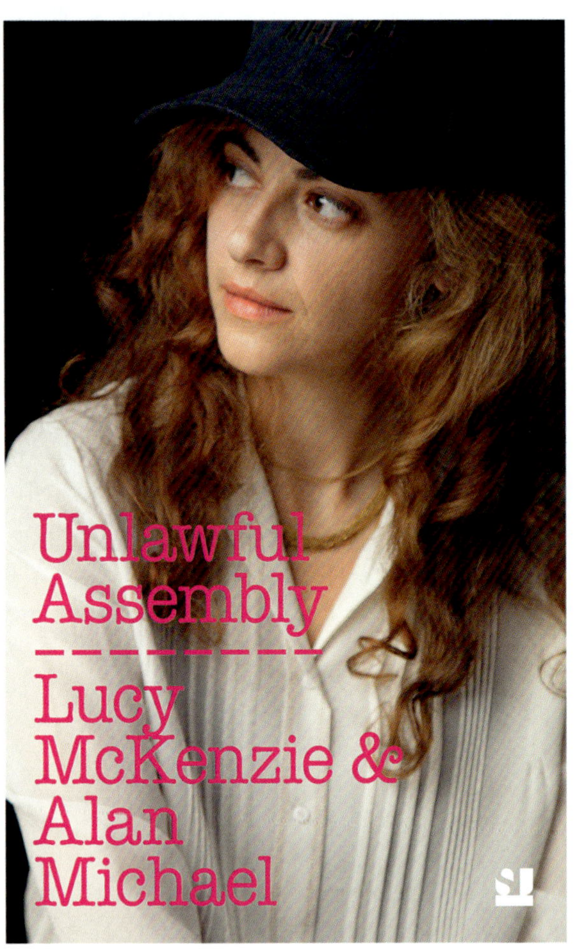
Unlawful
Assembly
Lucy
McKenzie &
Alan
Michael

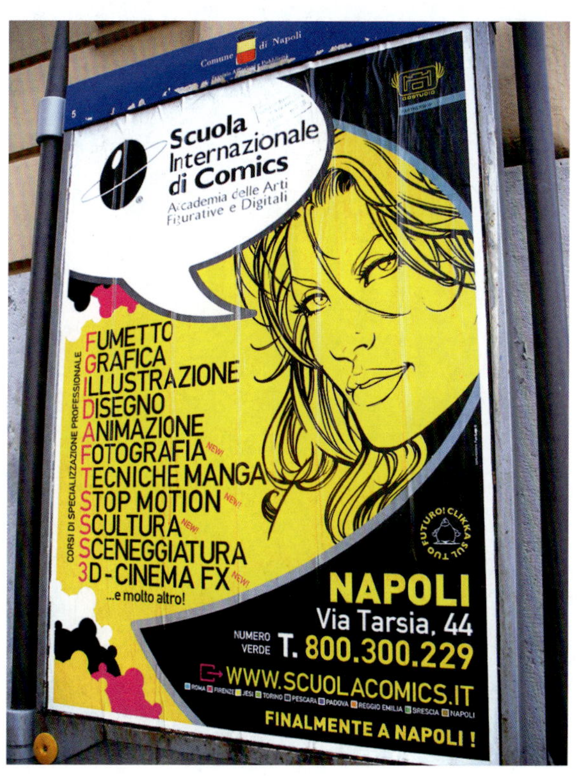
Comune di Napoli
Scuola Internazionale di Comics
Accademia delle Arti Figurative e Digitali
CORSI DI SPECIALIZZAZIONE PROFESSIONALE
FUMETTO
GRAFICA
ILLUSTRAZIONE
DISEGNO
ANIMAZIONE
FOTOGRAFIA NEW!
TECNICHE MANGA
STOP MOTION NEW!
SCULTURA NEW!
SCENEGGIATURA
3D-CINEMA FX NEW!
...e molto altro!
FUTURO! CLIKKA SUL TUO
NAPOLI
Via Tarsia, 44
NUMERO VERDE T. 800.300.229
WWW.SCUOLACOMICS.IT
ROMA FIRENZE JESI TORINO PESCARA PADOVA REGGIO EMILIA BRESCIA NAPOLI
FINALMENTE A NAPOLI !

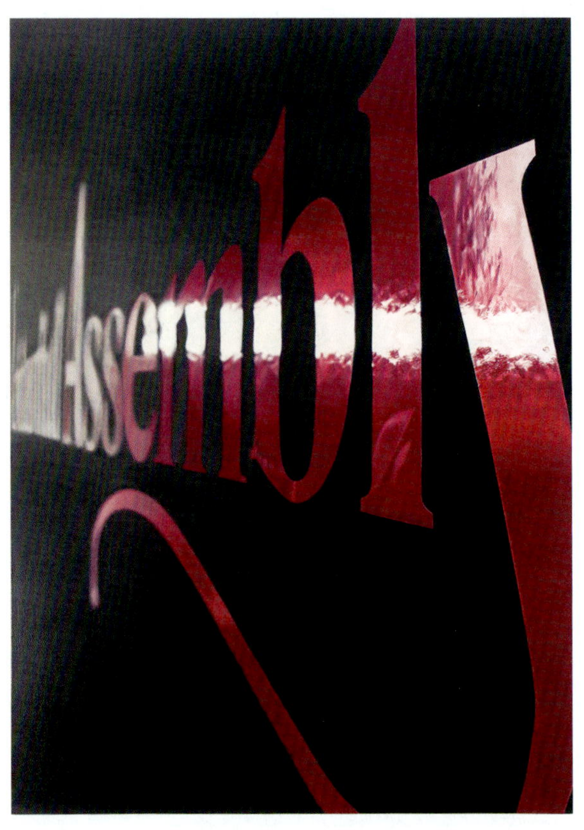

Alan Michael
Gases Rising, 2013, oil on canvas
Courtesy Vilma Gold

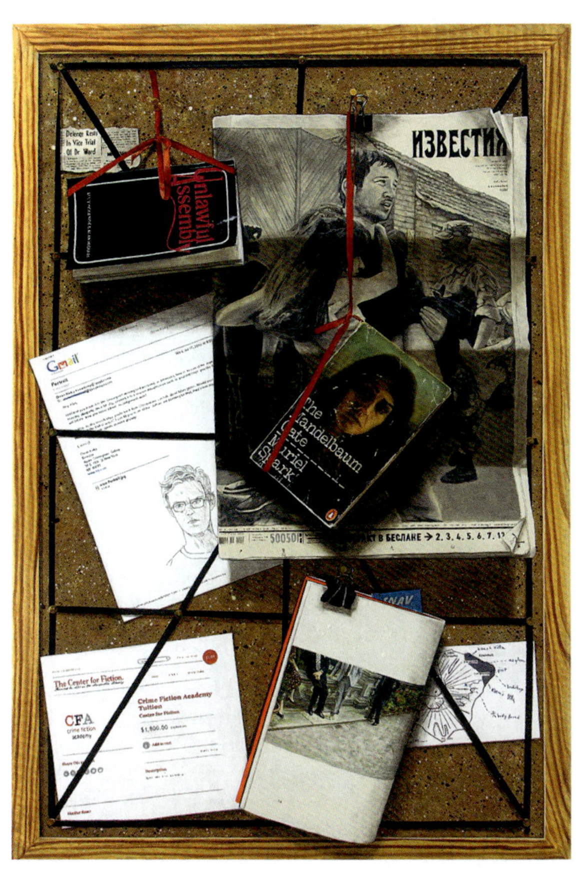

Lucy McKenzie
Quodlibet XXVII (Unlawful Assembly), 2013, oil on canvas
Private collection

There is nothing behind this book.

I often wonder why I surround myself with images, why they interest me so instinctively? Those flat things for coolly looking at, they're visible without reading, they speak into the presence and in that immediacy the absence/presence contradiction is resolved, which isn't true of writing.

One looks at a painting, one cannot look at a book. When one has read the book, what remains of it resembles what spoke in the immediacy of the object, but it's the object that questions reality. We tend to think that the visible and the real coincide… are the same. Now, it's obvious, though from evidence one must discover, that the visible and the real aren't identical. The visible is the real in representation, an instance of signification.

Bernard Noël

You have arrived in the room in which this story takes place. You pick up this book and it describes the room in which you are standing.

Holiday reading, like holiday romance, is an extension of fiction: the circumstances of the encounter are already inscribed in the situation you are about to experience.

You have arrived in this room, bags shed, distrustful of contrivance, both mechanical and strategic. This whole situation is booby-trapped, wound tight. You're suspicious of literature, of course, precisely because it arrives so appallingly on time! How *convenient* it is! How generic: how blindingly legible.

You're suspicious of everything, everyone. That the machinery of literature so intimately resembles that of criminal process makes suspects of us all; renders this book accessory. The Police Procedural is the exemplary literary genre: it is as close as we'll get to a timetable or a legend at the bottom of that literary map. Or an inventory of all the cogs and gears, the rigging, the prostheses, accents, weapons, greasepaint, wigs; protagonists, dotted about the landscape like vacated avatars.

A perverse hospitality is performed here on Stromboli. Your reclusive host, after all, is a man with a tattoo on his face which is an exact reproduction of his features. The implicit idea, you well understand, is *not* to unearth or exhume some expository cadaver, but to submit to that duplicitous resemblance composed on pages of hot, sun-kissed, sand-studded skin: forensic autopsy, you are reminded, is a convenient lie performed in legal and academic theatres. It has no place on Stromboli, in the shadow of this volcano. Do not disturb the sulphurous sand; leave the desiccated corpse of your friend buried and out of sight.

(Why are there more windows visible on the outside than you can find on the inside? Beyond, the sea is an idea of scalding sheet metal and the town is sketched crudely, inhabitants blurred, disinterested. Beyond, everything is heat-hazed into uncertainty, backdrop flapping in the sea breeze)

HERE (*), you are under the ascendant dictate of the image; the images dictate to you what you must say. Yes, the vision demands that you say all that it offers you and all that you find in it. You may close your eyes or leave them open, but if you close them you see something completely different from what actually happens: you see that of which you speak. It's precisely when you close your eyes to this room, to the visible Stromboli beyond, that literature pauses and waits—breath held in the dark beyond the shoreline—for your eyes to reopen and, with a start, begin reading and writing the spectacle again.

The key to the following texts is trompe l'oeil—is a *trompe l'oeil* key. And there is nothing behind this book.

Martin McGeown & Ed Atkins
London 2013

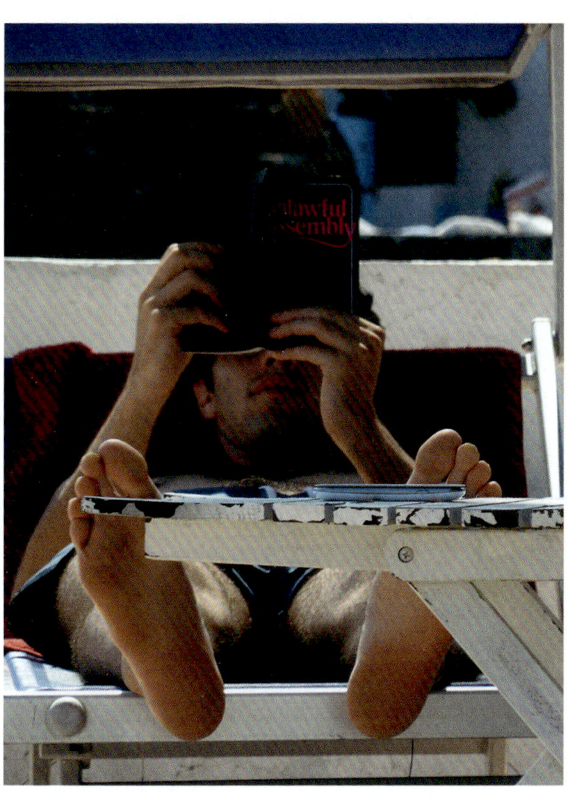

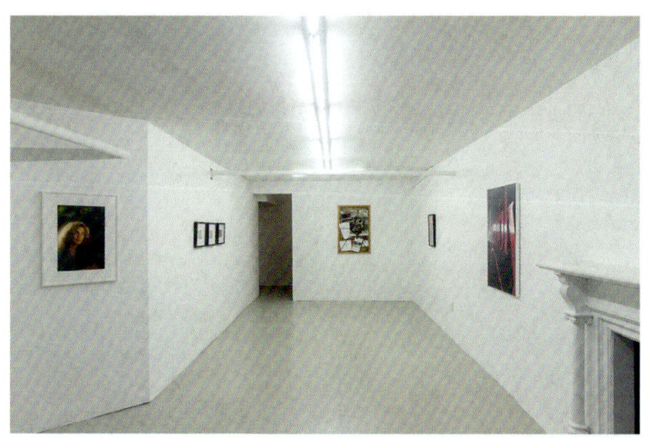

Note To Self, 2013
Installation view, The Artist's Institute

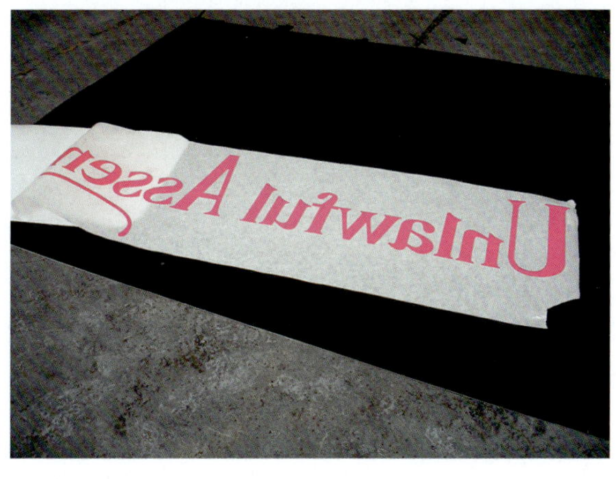
Unlawful Asse

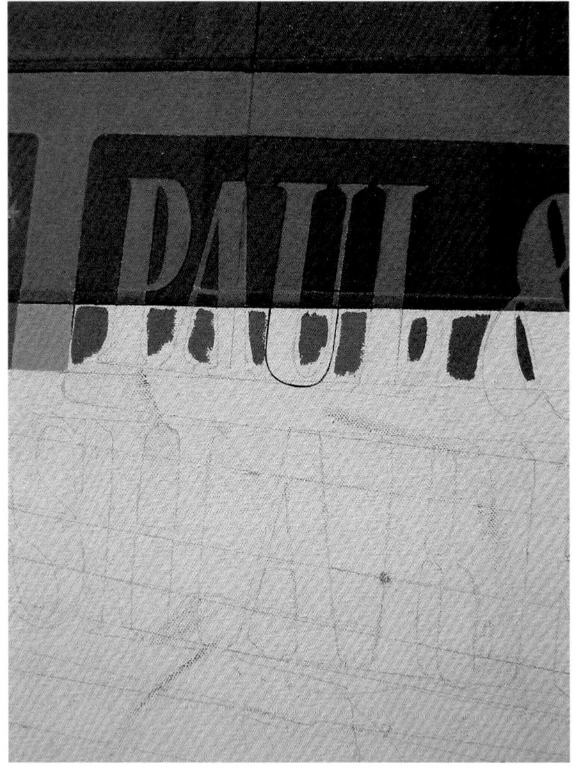

Alan Michael
Paul & Shark (detail), 2013, oil on canvas

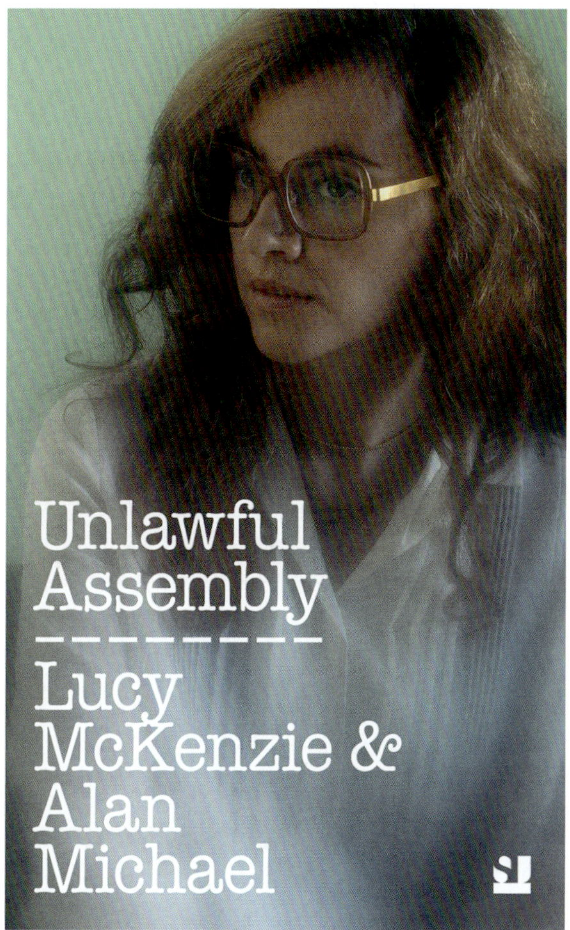
Unlawful
Assembly
Lucy
McKenzie &
Alan
Michael

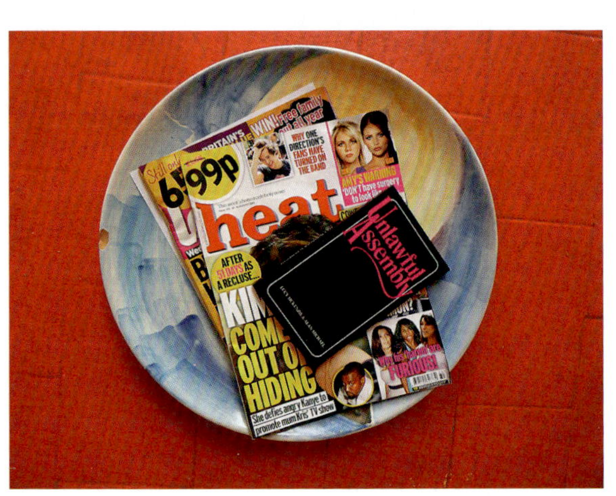

99p
heat
WHY ONE DIRECTION'S FANS HAVE TURNED ON THE BAND
AMY'S WARNING
AFTER 51 DAYS AS A RECLUSE...
HIDING
She defies angry Kanye to promote mum Kris' TV show
FURIOUS!
Unlawful Assembly

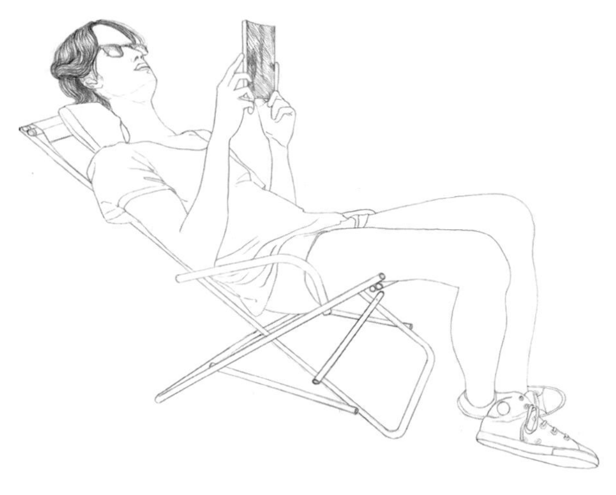

Lucy McKenzie
Untitled, 2013, pencil on paper
Courtesy the artist